Of Flat Earth and Protein Mania

Decoding Our Labyrinth of Biases

SOH SZE TIONG

First Published in Singapore
Copyright © 2026 Soh Sze Tiong
All rights reserved.

ISBN: 978-981-94-4552-3

*'We do not describe the world we see.
We see the world we can describe.'*

René Descartes

Contents

Acknowledgments

Preface   1

Approaching The Book   5

1   The Odyssey of Flat Earthers   7

2   A Youth's Radical Journey   11

3   Rich and Ripe for The Taking   15

Resilience Against Digital Predators   20

4   Gastronationalism   22

5   The Tote Stash   28

6   Smokescreens of Superfoods   32

Traditions and Myths of Appetite   38

7   SPH Media's Number Game   41

8   Anti-Social Anchors in Urban Planning   45

Growth-Fueled Biases   51

9   The Divine Oversight   55

10   The Identity Rabbit Hole   59

11   The Moral Dilemma of Right Versus Right   66

Of Biases and Prejudice   73

Repercussions of Biases   75

12   ExxonMobil's Foresight Trap   76

13   Lingering Ghosts of Colonialism   81

14   Sins of Inhospitality   90

15   A Price Tag on Ethics   97

16   The Architecture of Aversion   103

Decoding Our Biases   109

17   Decision-Making Biases   110

18   Social Perception Biases   116

19   Moral Biases   126

20   Emotional Biases   134

21	The Seven Mindshifts	140
22	A Creature of Context	142
23	A Disciple of Experience	146
24	A Collective Defender	152
25	A Dot Connector	156
26	A Nuanced Inquirer	160
27	An Equanimous Self-Steward	166
28	A Creative Renegade	170
	Parting Notes	174
	Credit, End Notes, and Reference	176

Acknowledgments

I owe my early love of words to my uncle Teck Kee, who entrusted me with his crossword puzzles. Many thanks to Jean Rosalind Vessey, who started a creative writing club at my secondary school and encouraged what was, at the time, my delusional attempt to become a writer. To Stefano Vinci, for treating my attempts at writing with a seriousness I have not yet learned to give myself. And to my primary school playmates, who let me take part in the burial of our classroom pet goldfish, which became a precious lesson in how quietly my own biases can feel like common sense.

Preface

My fascination with the architecture of human thought began at the age of seven, sparked by the death of a goldfish. The goldfish was one of the many inhabitants in our classroom aquarium. When it passed away, a group of well-meaning classmates decided to hold a burial for the goldfish, beneath a tree in the school compound. To mark the grave so that no other students would trample over it, they chose a rather puzzling fencing material. It was fish-shaped seafood-flavoured crackers. I found it both uncomfortable and insensitive that my peers would honour the poor creature with a snack, presumably made from its own kind. Without discussing with them, I removed the crackers when the ceremony ended. Shortly after, my classmates discovered what I did and accused me of intentionally 'desecrating' the burial spot. I was isolated from the playgroup for many weeks because of my action! I learned that very afternoon that what one may deem reasonable, another may deem absurd. It was my first real encounter with the complexity of interacting with others. What we perceive as 'universal truth' or logic is often nothing more than a personal perspective. That experience taught me about the unsettling but vital possibility that my thoughts and opinions are never the same as another's, and that assuming otherwise is the surest step toward misunderstanding.

For a long while, the lesson from the goldfish burial seemed to have little relevance to my life as a student or in the military. In school, we were only focused on a single academic goal: to graduate and find a well-paid job. In the military, we were trained to thrive on consensus; we were constantly reminded that deviating from the ethos of obeying all lawful orders could mean the difference between life and death. It wasn't until I entered the world of consultancy that the goldfish epiphany finally made sense. I had assumed consultants were hired primarily for their ability to frame problems well, but I quickly realised that possessing problem-solving skills was merely the tip of the iceberg. The excellence of a consultant lies in their ability to secure buy-in, implement the recommended solutions, and deliver measurable results. To achieve this, I had to guide stakeholders to see through my frame, which meant first understanding their 'mental scaffolding'. When I first took on the role of a consultant, my superior often advised me to identify all my stakeholders' red-button issues. Still, I quickly realised that knowing their triggers is useless if I don't understand why their triggers exist in the first place. Most stakeholders' red-button issues are often rooted in legacy structural problems, which are also sustained by stakeholders' biased perceptions. To address legacy issues in an organisation, I first had to understand the stakeholders' rationale.

The seeds for this book were actually sown while I was writing my first book, *Staying H.I.R.E.d - The Cultural Kingmaker's Guide to Building Work Oasis*. The content of *Staying H.I.R.E.d* was drawn from my experience building a sales team for my slow-fashion retail business, where I developed a system to foster effective followership and empower individuals at work to become change agents, advocates for a collaborative culture. However, as I mapped out the belief systems required for a thriving 'work oasis', I realised that an organisational framework is only as effective as the minds inhabiting it. The connection is clear: leadership begins in the architecture of the mind. For cultural leadership to truly take root, individuals must master meta-cognition, the ability to think about their own thinking. This is a skill as pertinent to an effective consultant as it is to an organisation's leader. Thus, I decided to follow up with a book dedicated to biases. Why biases? Biases are the direct consequence of our mental shortcuts. Understanding them is one of the fastest and most effective ways to discover how we truly think, and more importantly, how we can begin to think better.

I have structured this book as a series of essays divided into four distinct sections. We begin with real-world stories, examining them through the lens of biases. Then we explore the repercussions of these bias-led actions across four critical dimensions: the economic, political, social, and moral. After those essays, we move toward defining the specific biases that might have influenced the incidents discussed earlier. Finally, I present the mindshifts needed to cultivate greater awareness of our mental shortcuts. My goal is not to eliminate biases—our brains are evolutionarily hardwired to rely on cognitive shortcuts to process information efficiently, and therefore we are inherently biased—but to account for them and mitigate their consequences.

Of Flat Earth and Protein Mania is intended as an exercise in discovering and learning how biases influence the protagonists' decisions in the essays, so that we may identify the universal architecture of how we all think. By investigating the mental labyrinths others have wandered into, we may begin to recognise the same patterns in ourselves. I also want to draw on Hannah Arendt's theory of self-realisation: Arendt theorised that we learn who we truly are through our actions and speech in the public sphere. I believe we can also discover our inherent biases by observing our instinctive perceptions of the events discussed in these pages, turning the lens of inquiry back onto ourselves. These essays are intended to be mirrors, not judgments.

A caveat, however: my views are not objective reflections of reality; they are much clouded by prejudices and limited exposure, as are those of the subjects of these essays. Therefore, I ask that you do not read this like a textbook of truth. Instead, I hope it sparks curiosity on how and why we think the way we do. We may never fully grasp another person's mind, let alone our own. Nonetheless, seeking to understand the thought processes behind the actions described in the essays remains an effective effort toward greater discernment and metacognition.

This book is an invitation to join me in that detective work: analysing others' hints of thought to sharpen our discernment. I hope that as you turn these pages, you recognise your own invisible architecture of perceptions. May these essays allow you to build bridges where there were once awareness gaps you were oblivious to. That is the true journey I hope *Of Flat Earth and Protein Mania* will embark you on. Ultimately, recognising our biases reveals how deeply they shape our thinking and, most importantly, our ethics. I believe that by strengthening our metacognition, we might not only become more effective thinkers, but also better human beings.

Approaching This Book

This book can be approached in more than one way. The book is written for the reader to move through it sequentially, beginning with the stories in the first and second sections, which illustrate the subtle influence of cognitive shortcuts on human judgment and their repercussions. After that, it leads the reader to the third section, which examines the specific biases that may have influenced the events described in the preceding chapters. And finally, to the section on mindshifts, perspectives to cultivate for greater awareness of the tendencies in our own thinking.

You may also find the stories useful as prompts for group discussion for workplace training. Examining how the individuals in each narrative might have reasoned through their decisions can reveal how differently people interpret the same events. Such conversations often surface hidden assumptions and offer a practical way to discover how we think.

Ultimately, this book is not meant to prescribe any definitive answers. It is intended as an invitation to examine how we perceive, interpret, and judge the world around us.

1
The Odyssey of Flat Earthers

In the spring of 2020, as much of the world stood still under pandemic lockdowns, a curious and somewhat tragic story emerged from Italy. As reported by *Newsweek* on September 1, 2020, in an article titled 'Flat Earthers Quarantined After Taking Wrong Route Trying to Find End of the World', a middle-aged couple from Venice, convinced that the Earth was flat, defied quarantine orders to set sail for what they believed was the edge of the world. Their goal was to reach Lampedusa, an island south of Sicily, which in their minds marked the boundary of Earth's flat terrain. The pair sold their car to fund their expedition. Ironically, they used a compass to navigate. The compass is a device that relies on Earth's magnetic field (terrestrial magnetism) for navigation. The Earth's magnetic field is generated by a spherical planet, which thus contradicts the Flat-Earthers' beliefs. It was a short-lived expedition; the couple ended up, exhausted and lost, on Ustica, a small island northwest of their intended destination. They were caught and quarantined by the authorities. Determined to get to what they believed was the world's edge, they attempted to escape multiple times.

As readers learning about the couple's experiences from a news article, we have the advantage of being observers and can easily recognise that the couple's actions were illogical and unreasonable. However, for the couple, their repeated attempts to escape and their continued pursuit of the doomed expedition attested to their insistence on clinging to their beliefs. Remaining committed to beliefs, even when they are harmful, is a trap that any of us can fall into. In the couple's case, their entrenched conviction led them not only to a failed expedition but also to ignore a glaring logical inconsistency: relying on a compass to navigate an expedition founded on the theory that the Earth is flat. The Italian couple's story is an insightful example of how our views can be clouded by biases, leading us to overlook facts and evidence that could prove our thinking is flawed.

The belief that the Earth is flat is not a new phenomenon but has historical roots dating back to the 19th century. Actually, ancient societies held flat-Earth views, but it was Samuel Rowbotham, from Cambridgeshire, England, who revived and popularised the modern flat-Earth theory in his 19th-century writings, *Zetetic Astronomy: Earth Not a Globe*. Rowbotham was likely motivated by his religious beliefs and a desire to dismantle Isaac Newton's legacy on universal gravitation. In a *BBC* article by Camay Chapman-Cameron, Rowbotham conducted his critical experiment in Old Bedford River, a straight waterway on a flat marshland region between Cambridgeshire and Norfolk. Rowbotham asserted that if he could see a boat's flag through a telescope for its entire journey to Welney in Norfolk, it would prove the world was flat. In fact, he claimed to have seen the flag all the way to Welney Bridge, six miles from his starting location. The experiment was repeated and served as his primary evidence for the next three decades, during which he gave lectures to propagate his beliefs. His zeal paid off when John Hampden, captivated and convinced by his work, continued promoting the flat-Earth theory. This historical account of the flat-Earth theory shows how easily our understanding of reality can be shaped and distorted.

During the Victorian era, the flat-Earth theory was a fringe belief held by a handful of individuals. In our present times, this theory has resurged as an internet-fueled conspiracy, whose spread is aided by social media algorithms. In a *CNN* report titled 'The flat-Earth conspiracy is spreading around the globe. Does it hide a darker core? A *YouGov* survey in the U.S. suggested that as many as 1 in 6 Americans are not entirely certain the world is round. A similar survey conducted in Brazil found that 7% rejected the concept of a spherical Earth. The theory's widespread growth is aided by the ease with which information spreads online, uniting a community of flat-earth believers. The unbridled spread of information on the internet has also spawned a proliferation of factions and theories surrounding the flawed refutation of a spherical Earth.

The popularity of the flat-earth theory may suggest an undercurrent in our society. According to Daniel Jolley, a senior lecturer in the psychology of conspiracy theories, who was interviewed in the CNN report, people who subscribe to these theories are often trying to make sense of the world, but unfortunately, through a biased lens. Their adherence to conspiracy theories, which we may view as preposterous, could stem from deep-seated distrust of governments, scientific institutions, or even the mainstream media. Their mistrust often arises from feeling let down or marginalised in society. For individuals who feel unheard or isolated, unconventional theories offer a compelling alternative framework that fosters a sense of belonging, validates their worldview, and empowers them to speak up in situations where they might otherwise be silenced.

Conspiracy theories thrive significantly in social climates characterised by a lack of trust and fairness. They serve as a coping mechanism for individuals facing anxiety, uncertainty, and disempowerment. A conspiracy theory functions as a psychological balm, allowing believers to feel smarter than they would if they accepted the mainstream view, and giving them an ego boost. In a way, it provides believers with a sense of purpose and community;

those enticing emotional rewards of belonging outweigh any need for factual correction. In the case of the Venetian couple, their expedition was motivated by strongly held, possibly emotionally anchored beliefs, which led them to willingly incur personal costs and risks. Their drift off course is a symptom of a broader societal phenomenon: a fraying social fabric that drives individuals to seek alternative narratives as an attempt to restore a sense of control.

By dismissing Flat-Earthers or any conspiracists as irrational outliers, we are missing the true reason why and how easily we all can fall prey to our own cognitive biases. Cognitive biases are not confined to the fringes of society; they are a universal feature of the human mind that affects every one of us. Often subtle, biases influence high-stakes decisions in boardrooms, political ideologies, and our everyday social interactions. While the couple's expedition may seem like an anomaly, the cognitive patterns they exhibited may be strikingly familiar to our own. If it isn't about the shape of the Earth, it's likely about religion, race, identity, or even our personal financial decisions. In some form, we all carry narratives we wish to be true, and we may consciously or unconsciously seek out signs to confirm them, sometimes even at the risk of getting lost along the way.

2
A Youth's Radical Journey

In the digital era, traditional barriers like distance and elite access to knowledge have largely dissolved, placing unprecedented amounts of information within immediate reach. This ease of access to information offers youths a unique opportunity to transcend the limits of their formative networks, such as family and school. For them, our modern digital landscape is a vast intellectual frontier that easily enables them to build a more objective, diverse understanding of the world. However, the tragic case of Michael Alexander Gloss, a 21-year-old American who ended up fighting for Russia in the Ukraine war, tells a troubling reality: our digital ecosystem also serves as a breeding ground for our biases, as it is a tool for overcoming them. And unfortunately, young individuals who are more frequently connected to the internet, such as Michael Alexander Gloss, are often exposed to a torrent of misinformation aimed at influencing or, even worse, radicalising them.

Gloss's tragic trajectory was reported in *The Guardian,* in the article 'Son of CIA deputy director was killed while fighting for Russia'. The article mentioned that Gloss, the son of a high-ranking

CIA official, was killed fighting under contract for the Russian military in Ukraine in 2024. His bizarre transformation from a youth who advocated for human rights and the environment to a mercenary soldier fighting against Ukraine warns us of the dangers of online radicalisation that prey on young people who were innocently searching for meaning in their lives.

Gloss's journey was particularly striking due to his seemingly self-contradictory transition into a pro-Russian mercenary. Initially, he was an idealist, actively involved in progressive circles that advocate for gender equality and environmental protection. He then travelled to Turkey to help victims of a devastating earthquake. All his actions embodied a youth who clearly desired to contribute positively to the world. Yet this promising humanist adopted a radical ideological shift in supporting Russia's military actions against Ukraine. It was an unexpected stance for someone regarded as progressive. Gloss's tragic end is likely a consequence of radicalisation tactics, which often prey on victims' cognitive vulnerabilities. Young internet users are particularly susceptible due to their still-developing critical judgment. Youths' reliance on mental shortcuts and stereotypes to make quick decisions in social situations often leads them to readily absorb biased messages with limited critical filters.

A plausible explanation for Gloss's drastic decision to join Russia's contingent could be social isolation and exposure to radical content, both online and offline. It was reported that while abroad in Turkey, Gloss was growingly frustrated with U.S. foreign policy, particularly its support of Israel during the Gaza conflict. Could his frustration with his government fuel polarised anti-government views? Did his anti-government stance lead him to ally with Russia? Perhaps fighting in the Russian army was, in his view, an ideological battle against U.S. imperialism and its associated harms? We will not be able to ascertain Gloss's rationale for his behaviours. Whichever the truth, it is likely, as with most radicalised youths, that Gloss was unfortunately lured into a rabbit hole of misleading or distorted narratives while earnestly seeking ideas and information that might deepen or structure his ideals and causes. His entrapment in a cloud of misinformation might have increasingly disconnected him from the mainstream news and information.

Internet platforms are designed to maximise engagement. The same systems also amplify misinformation, forming echo chambers of conspiracy theories and cherry-picked facts. Young people, often seeking meaning, identity, and a sense of belonging, are particularly vulnerable. Such digital enclaves can significantly skew perceptions, leading users to mistake distortions for truth. During his time in Turkey, Gloss was reported to have become increasingly anti-American and anti-Western, and to have been drawn to conspiracy theories. Gloss's acquaintance believed that his deepening anger and disillusionment with the U.S. might have been amplified by conspiracy theory videos he watched, which led him to pro-Russian views.

For Gloss, what might begin as an innocuous personal grievance against his country slowly metastasised into a dangerous ideology. Gloss likely justified his radical shift by aligning himself with causes he perceived as a necessary opposition to what he saw as corrupt or harmful actions; in his case, the United States's stance on the Israel-Gaza conflict. Fighting for Russia may have embodied that moral counterbalance he sought. Daniel Jolley, the senior lecturer in the psychology of conspiracy theories, suggests that radicalisation often stems from an innate human drive to play a productive role in the world. When that motivation is guided through a biased lens, it may lead individuals astray. Gloss's radicalised journey is one such sobering example. Yet his case isn't an isolated one; it's part of a larger social phenomenon in which victims who feel disconnected or disillusioned are particularly vulnerable to extreme ideologies disseminated through the digital ecosystem. But the digital ecosystem is not solely to blame. Social isolation also makes one more susceptible to extremism and conspiracies. A safeguard against radicalisation is to ensure a social environment that encourages open, critical discourse on diverse views and opinions.

Misinformation in the digital ecosystem is complex and constantly evolving. Therefore, curbing it requires governments, platforms, schools, and families all pulling in the same direction. This also raises the question of whether stronger safeguards should be imposed on technology companies, independent of free speech arguments, requiring them to be accountable for mitigating public risks, protecting individuals' privacy, and safeguarding democratic processes. However, digital policing alone is insufficient; it must be complemented with social re-engagement to break the isolation that drives individuals like Gloss toward radical echo chambers. Most importantly, schools and communities should consider curricula and grassroots activities that foster cognitive resilience. To do so, they ought to consider providing youth and adults with safe, non-discriminatory spaces where they can engage with diverse perspectives and learn to critically challenge biases that make one vulnerable to harmful ideologies.

3
Rich and Ripe for The Taking

In May 2025, the *Financial Times* published a striking exposé on Singapore: a nation globally recognised for its affluence, orderliness, and efficiency had become the world's most heavily scammed nation per capita. On average, each victim loses over US$4,000. The *Financial Times* described the phenomenon as a 'scamdemic', presumably referring to the unprecedentedly high incidences of scams. In that context, I believe calling it a 'scamdemic' also highlights endemic factors in Singapore that might have caused the flare-up. Could trustworthy governance and reliable infrastructure have turned Singapore into a fertile ground for scammers?

A notable element of the report was how easily highly educated and seemingly discerning citizens were deceived. According to a report from the *National Technological University*, Singapore boasts a literacy rate of 97%. And according to *Statista,* 43.3% of Singapore's labour force holds a university degree or higher as of 2024. Singapore's high incidence of scams among the educated proved a point: as surreal or counterintuitive as it may seem, associating high levels of education with immunity to scams is itself a biased perspective. It might also be precisely why many Singaporeans are vulnerable to scams: being educated, they may not believe they could be easy targets. In fact, it is well known that many scam victims are often quietly confident that it wouldn't happen to them and let their guard down as a result. Besides being too overconfident, could socio-environmental factors also make Singaporeans relatively susceptible to scams? A plausible theory of Singaporeans' vulnerability may lie in cognitive biases, such as the automation and authority biases. Singapore's socio-political environment, one that emphasises top-down efficiency, strict legislation, and high-visibility policing, may foster automation and authority biases among its citizens.

Singaporeans live in one of the most efficient societies in the world, where even its bureaucracy is digitised. Efficiency is Singapore's national ethos. In an environment where infrastructure is consistently reliable, individual vigilance can erode over time. Because Singapore's infrastructure is widely credited to competent governance, many citizens may assume that all government-run automated systems are inherently secure. Here lies the crux of Singaporeans' vulnerability: their automation bias made them less likely to scrutinise any calls or messages that seemed to be part of a trusted, efficient system. When scam victims receive messages from recognised institutions bearing a familiar government logo, or from callers whose voices mimic an official tone, it is often all it takes to win victims' trust and confidence. Because of Singaporeans' unfaltering trust in their institutional infrastructure, anything presented within its familiar codes may be easily mistaken as trustworthy.

Another likely factor contributing to Singaporeans' vulnerability is their predisposition to ascribe credibility and correctness to figures of authority. This trust is rooted in Singapore's political history and internalised through upbringing and education. Since the country's independence, the ruling party has meticulously cultivated a narrative of the infallible integrity of its political members. It often reinforces it with cautionary tales about corruption in other countries and distinguishes itself as an incorruptible government. The ruling party's theory of tying high ministerial salaries to attract talented lawmakers and deterring corruption and greed is readily and well accepted across many generations. Overall, the ruling party's messages have been remarkably effective, cultivating strong, deeply ingrained trust in its governance.

Singapore is also often described as a 'nanny state' due to the government's pervasive guidance in citizens' lives. This form of 'helicopter parenting' on a national scale was, in the ruling party's belief, a proactive way to ensure social stability and public welfare. But the extensive social engineering and regulation might, over time, diminish the development of individual critical discernment. As citizens become accustomed to the state managing risks and issuing clear directives, their scepticism subsides. Additionally, Singapore's efficient and strict policing has led to a long-standing record of low crime, and it might also inadvertently make Singaporeans less vigilant. This may be precisely how scammers have deceived victims by impersonating police officers, government officials, and even personnel from Singapore's Anti-Scam Centre, with alarming success. Due to authority bias, Singaporeans are more likely to obey and comply when they encounter a person in authority, making them easy targets for impersonators. With the emergence of artificial intelligence tools, scam tactics, such as deepfake videos of trusted authorities with unprecedented realism, will become increasingly sophisticated and dangerous in capitalising on victims' entrenched authority bias.

If these patterns hold, they reveal a deep vulnerability in the Singaporean psyche. It also raises a difficult question: Could Singapore's longstanding emphasis on rote learning, combined with information distributed through centralised news media, have created epistemic dependency among its people? Could this reliance on authority for knowledge lead the population to inadvertently develop a naivety that leaves them ill-equipped to navigate the complexities of unmanaged information? In such an environment, Singaporeans may have had limited opportunities to regularly exercise their critical thinking skills. That might have given rise to generations that outsource critical thinking and passively consume information. Trusting external authority for knowledge, while considered essential for social stability, can become a profoundly dangerous aspect of modern life. In a chaotic digital ecosystem characterised by rapid information proliferation, false, biased, or manipulated narratives can be widely adopted. With social media and messaging platforms now functioning as media channels in their own right, there are more conduits for receiving information and for exposure to persuasion, distortion, and manipulation. While stricter policing may deter scams, Singapore's Achilles' heel may well be its citizens' instinct to trust rather than verify information.

Another revelation about Singapore from scams is the prevalence of those involving romantic relationships. Romance scams unveil an often-overlooked cost of Singapore's hyper-competitive ethos, which might have precipitated a sense of inadequacy among emotionally brittle or lonely individuals. Victims may find it easier to seek intimacy and validation in the virtual realm within the privacy of their homes, where their vulnerabilities are not exposed. In their earnest longing for affection and attention, they became easy prey to expert scammers.

In response to the rise in scamming incidents, the Singapore government introduced several stringent laws and frameworks, including mandatory caning of offenders in 2025. It is a positive step that serves as a stern deterrent to would-be scammers and their money mules. My only caution about the approach: amplifying policing efforts and increasing the weight of accountability on financial and communication institutions may, counterintuitively, reinforce citizens' belief that the government has and will continue to protect them from all harm. It may once again perpetuate a bias toward unquestioning obedience to authority. Scam syndicates are decentralised, operating persistently on a layered 'cell-based' transnational structure involving anonymous actors. Given how quickly scam operatives have evolved, punitive measures against scammers may not be implemented effectively. From this perspective, in addition to issuing punitive laws to deter scammers, Singapore ought to address the socio-political factors that foster cognitive vulnerabilities among its citizens, vulnerabilities that make them easy targets in the first place.

Singapore's long record of effective governance has cultivated strong public trust, unintentionally conditioning its people to be under-discerning. The nation's intense 'rat race' culture and its glorification of perfection have also isolated emotionally brittle and vulnerable individuals. This internal fragility within Singaporean society is a strategic liability in a new social order marked by chaotic information flow. A vast web of misinformation, embedded in the digital ecosystem and turbocharged by AI, threatens societies and governments. As observed in global events such as the British Brexit referendum and subsequent US elections, disinformation spreads deliberately to destabilise societies. In the end, a citizen who questions what they read or hear is more protective against the spread of misinformation than any law. This creates a difficult tension for the Singapore government: how does it foster discerning, critical citizens capable of fending off scammers and disinformation proxies, while ensuring they remain compliant with its centralised power, which has long enabled it to execute policies and implement legislation swiftly?

Resilience Against Digital Predators

In today's interconnected world, information flows ceaselessly from computer screens and mobile devices, offering us unprecedented access to knowledge and diverse viewpoints. The digital age empowers individuals to form well-rounded opinions; presumably, we are more adept at challenging established narratives and thinking critically about global issues. Yet the exponential abundance of information has proven to be a double-edged sword. The very social platforms designed to connect us to a volume of data are now breeding grounds for bias and disinformation. This is because to facilitate rapid access to information, these networks often prioritise viral content over accuracy. Our reliance on digital content for information may have led to a decline in our critical reasoning skills, making us even more vulnerable to misinformation and deception. The emergence of artificial intelligence (AI) has significantly accelerated the speed, scale, and sophistication of misinformation tactics, raising serious ethical concerns about its use. Human perception, naturally prone to bias, is now even more susceptible to external exploitation.

The tragicomic odyssey of flat-earthers, the radicalisation of activist Michael Gloss, and the pervasive scams in Singapore collectively expose a troubling reality: our internet age has enabled a wide range of deception tactics. The stories illustrate how easily reality can be distorted and how quickly societal trust can erode. In all three stories, agents of misinformation, ranging from transnational crime syndicates seeking financial gain to state-sponsored propagandists aiming for social destabilisation, exploit our most humane needs for belonging and trust. These agents treat the digital realm as a battleground to prey on victims' cognitive vulnerabilities and to disseminate misleading narratives to influence the victims' behaviours. Whether their goal is ideological warfare or financial deceit, these agents are relentless in exploiting our cognitive biases.

To safeguard humanity, we must safeguard a digital future against malicious agents of deception. Building resilience against the ills of the digital age requires more than technological solutions or regulatory legislation. We need an approach that strikes a delicate balance: leveraging the vast advantages of digital technology without neglecting human connections, because engaging with each other is the most powerful antidote to social isolation, a condition that reinforces personal biases. Democratic governments must invest in structured, accessible, and transparent platforms through which residents can participate in decision-making processes. Whether their participation is through traditional town halls or digital platforms, the purpose of these initiatives is to enable community members and local officials to work together. By strengthening local dialogue and community engagement, we may restore social connections and counter loneliness and isolation, which are so easily exploited by deception.

4
Gastronationalism

Alberto Grandi, an Italian professor of economic history and food historian at the University of Parma, sparked widespread controversy in Italy when he claimed, in a Financial Times interview, that the beloved Roman dish Carbonara is, in fact, of American origin. According to Grandi, the origin of Carbonara is a culinary fusion adapted for American soldiers in Italy after World War II. He stoked further anger by suggesting that the most authentic Parmesan cheese today may not be found in Italy, but in Wisconsin. The interview was published just as the Italian government was campaigning for its cuisine to be recognised by UNESCO as an element of intangible cultural heritage. For the ruling party and many Italians, Grandi's assertions felt like a direct affront to Italy's cultural legacy and a betrayal at a pivotal diplomatic moment.

Grandi's comments weren't mere conjectures; they drew on existing academic literature and historical sources that traced patterns of food migration. Notably, he explained that Carbonara was first concocted in 1944 by an Italian chef for American soldiers in Riccione, using their army rations of bacon and powdered eggs. Another of his controversial claims concerns Parmigiano Reggiano. Parmigiano Reggiano is famously produced in the Emilia-Romagna region of Italy, where medieval monks first crafted it between the cities of Parma and Reggio Emilia. According to Grandi, Italian immigrants who began making Parmesan in Wisconsin in the early 20th century were the producers who actually preserved the original production methods. Meanwhile, the recipe in Parma, Italy, has evolved to the present-day product, known for its intense aroma and flavour. The production of Parmigiano Reggiano cheese is strictly regulated and occurs only in the provinces of Parma, Reggio Emilia, Modena, Bologna, and Mantua. For Italians who regard Parmigiano Reggiano as a symbol of Italy's gastronomic pride, Grandi's revelation is hard to swallow.

The indignant uproar he provoked was not an intellectual rebuttal over historical facts, but rather a Pavlovian reflex, an instinctive lashing out triggered by a perceived threat to Italy's identity. Lacking any counterevidence to invalidate Grandi's theory, critics' anger manifested as a visceral defence of the deeply cherished myth that Italian dishes originated solely and purely in Italy, uncontaminated by external influences from trade, migration, or cultural exchange.

Some right-wing politicians who frame Italian cuisine as a cornerstone of the nation's sovereign identity were quick to seize that moment, turning Grandi's interview into a political flashpoint. Matteo Salvini, Italy's deputy prime minister and leader of the far-right League, who has long wielded food as a symbol of nationalist identity, publicly dismissed Grandi's assertions as stemming from his envy of Italians' discernment in taste and aesthetics. It was a perplexing accusation, given that Grandi is himself Italian. Salvini intensified his polemics by urging Italians to buy only Italian products. As a result, public discourse on Grandi's findings swiftly shifted from food history to gastronationalism, a murky political tactic that turns cuisine into a symbol of cultural purity.

What was missed in that heated, almost divisive reaction was that Grandi was not at all implying that Carbonara or Parmigiano Reggiano are not authentically Italian. All he intended was to draw our attention to the fact that many dishes we often deem 'traditional' are actually re-inventions and the result of rich cross-cultural exchange. Besides Carbonara and Parmigiano Reggiano cheese, he also shared that tiramisu and panettone are relatively modern creations, and pizza, a global icon closely associated with Italy today, wasn't even widespread in Italy until after World War II. Grandi emphasised that our fixed ideas about culinary traditions and authenticity are often established much later, after the dishes have already undergone significant evolution. Many Italian culinary traditions are the result of a constructed identity; 'Italian cuisine,' he provocatively argued, 'is more American than it is Italian.'

This phenomenon of gastronationalism, in which food heritage is defensively shielded from the notion that traditional cuisine often evolves through exchange and migration, is not unique to Italy. A strikingly similar tension exists in Southeast Asia, where netizens from both Singapore and Malaysia repeatedly clashed over the 'ownership' of their shared hawker food heritage. When Singapore announced its intention to nominate its hawker food culture for UNESCO status, many Malaysians took it as a direct slight, accusing Singapore of attempting to claim what was rightfully Malaysian. In reality, both countries share deep historical roots and parallel evolutions in their street food offerings.

The hawker-food rivalry began as digital banter. Malaysian netizens joked that their hawker fare is grittier, more flavorful, and less 'sanitised', implying greater authenticity than the bland versions in Singapore. Singaporeans, in turn, pointed to their Michelin-starred hawker stalls as evidence of culinary excellence, a passive-aggressive jab at their neighbour. Although most comments were trivial, some reflected netizens' nationalist stance on the ownership of hawker-food traditions. Unfortunately, when we chest-beat and argue defensively over the authenticity and ownership of food traditions, we often take our attention away from the reality that cuisines evolve and, in doing so, reflect society's ever-changing identity.

Gastronationalism in Italy also illustrated how it can have detrimental consequences for real-world policy. On March 29, 2023, in a *BBC* article titled 'Italy moves to ban lab-grown meat to protect food heritage', the Italian right-wing government championed a bill to ban laboratory-produced meat and other synthetic foods. Their motivation, as articulated by Francesco Lollobrigida, Minister for Agriculture and Food Sovereignty, and Prime Minister Giorgia Meloni, is to 'protect Italian food heritage and health'. The bill was presented as a defence of the nation's Mediterranean diet, and the ban won the support of powerful farmers' lobbies, such as Coldiretti.

Italy's ban on lab meat, ostensibly to preserve the nation's cultural purity, stood in stark contrast to nations already embracing global scientific advancement in lab-grown meat. Countries such as the US and Singapore have already approved lab-grown chicken for consumption, and the European Commission has suggested that cell-based agriculture could be a 'promising and innovative solution' for sustainable food systems. Instead, the Italian governing coalition weaponised the conviction that Italy's culinary tradition is inherently superior and must be protected at all costs to stir nationalistic emotions. They sacrificed Italy's progress in food technology for their political gain. Italy's move against lab-grown meat clearly illustrates how a seemingly harmless cultural bias can have profound implications, stifling a nation's strategic growth and long-term development.

Without the ban, companies and entrepreneurs in Italy could have capitalised on an emerging industry: Italy, a country renowned for its culinary expertise, could have played a leading role in thoughtful, regulated experimentation in alternative food production. Such a move could contribute to climate change solutions and food security while equally modernising the globally recognised 'Made in Italy' brand. Instead, Prime Minister Giorgia Meloni chose to leverage the populists' ingrained cultural bias for her political ends, thereby hampering any potential to establish Italy's global presence in modern food production.

Arguments over the provenance or origin of a national dish are rarely about unravelling the historical truth; almost always, they are about identity and ownership. Politicians frequently exploit this emotional confusion, presenting food as an unchanging, sacred marker of national culture that must be defended at all costs. Such a narrative easily stirs fierce nationalist fervour and secures electoral support by appealing directly to voters' cultural pride. What gastronationalism does is weaponise food and its traditions, a universally educative and unifying subject, to promulgate an inward-looking ideology.

Gastronationalism is, by and large, a manifestation of ownership bias, our ingrained human tendency to claim exclusive rights to cultural elements, motivated by a perceived superiority. An ownership-driven view of food as a national identity creates a rigid perspective that clashes with the dynamic and fluid nature of culinary culture. Gastronationalism is also bolstered by confirmation bias, a cognitive bias that compels one to seek out information that validates pre-existing beliefs. Both biases obscure the true evolution of all cuisines, which often carry narratives far more intriguing than any myth of purity.

The evolution of cuisine tells a story of how diverse flavours and ingredients, introduced through cultural encounters, are constantly adapted to unite and sustain communities. The spicy chilli fruit, indispensable in Thai, Indian, and Mexican cuisine, originated in the Americas. Sugar, a cornerstone of many Asian desserts, is a byproduct of colonial plantation economies. The Portuguese sponge cake inspired Japanese Kasutera cakes. Filipino *Adobo*, Peruvian *Ceviche*, and even the Southern European and Latin American *Empanada* owe their forms to centuries of colonial encounters, intricate trade routes, and diasporic reinvention. Every national dish reflects cultural exchanges and adaptations.

Ultimately, what makes a national dish meaningful is not its immutable, pure origin, but its continuous evolution and its remarkable ability to adapt to new hands, new tastes, and new contexts across cultures. Insisting on culinary purity as a proxy for a nation's identity is a biased perspective that erases the rich tapestry of human exchange embodied in a traditional dish. Every traditional dish, in its own way, is a shared inheritance, the result of centuries of adaptation, migration, and human ingenuity. Whether it is your national dish or mine, each is a testament to humans' collective journey.

5

The Tote Stash

In recent years, the image of the eco-conscious shopper carrying a canvas tote, wheeling past the organic food aisle, or strolling through farmers' markets, has become an aspirational portrait of young urban consumers. TikTokers have since distilled this image into a specific male archetype: the 'performative male', also known as the 'matcha man', which became a viral sensation in the spring of 2025. Unsurprisingly, the performative male is almost always carrying a canvas tote. The widespread adoption of canvas totes as reusable grocery bags is a clear and positive signal of rising consumer awareness of the environmental impact of their purchasing choices. Concurrently, the canvas tote has also evolved into a social signifier, an accessory that projects the user's commitment to specific social and political affiliations. The frenzy among Gen Z in the US to acquire Trader Joe's mini pastel canvas tote bags, or the widespread sight of individuals in Milan proudly sporting a 'New Yorker' tote bag, is evidence that these simple carriers have become coveted accessories with significant cultural cachet.

Uma Karmarkar and Bryan Bollinger, through their research focusing on consumer decision-making and psychology, discovered an interesting behaviour of shoppers who brought their own tote bags when buying groceries. In their study, they observed that these shoppers were more likely to buy organic produce and eco-friendly items and yet were also more likely to reward themselves by purchasing less healthy products, such as cookies, crisps, or ice cream. According to the study, the canvas tote may serve dual purposes for the tote-carrying shoppers: as a functional, sustainable carrier for their groceries and as a social signal of their ethical and cultural alignment. That potent psychological combination of genuinely adhering to a virtue and social signalling, according to the researchers, may encourage shoppers to indulge in ways that contradict the very values they outwardly project: as eco- and health-conscious consumers.

The shoppers' paradoxical indulgence can be attributed to a cognitive phenomenon known as the licensing effect, also called moral licensing. When people perceive their actions as morally or socially commendable, such as using a reusable bag to reduce waste, they may feel they have accrued 'moral credit' that entitles them to a subsequent indulgence or 'break'. For the shoppers in the study, using a reusable grocery bag, buying organic foods, or both could have encouraged them to make high-calorie junk food purchases. I can attest to that behaviour. I follow a vegetarian diet at home and always bring reusable totes when I shop for groceries. I would often reach for a bag or two of crisps as a treat, but only after silencing my nagging guilt over my unhealthy choice. To do so, I justify my indulgence by my adherence to a vegetarian diet, which I take to be presumably healthier and more environmentally sustainable, even though I know that is not entirely true.

The other, more intriguing, finding from the research was that when store policy made reusable bags mandatory and required shoppers to use them, their paradoxical behaviour of indulging in unhealthy treats disappeared. This key detail suggests that when a virtuous act is mandated rather than self-directed, the act ceases to be a personal moral investment. Unlike voluntary deeds, mandatory positive actions do not evoke 'moral licensing'. The finding implies that self-licensing bias often leads to inconsistent ethical behaviour, sometimes with profound societal implications. This same cognitive lapse is often a leading cause of the downfall of transformative leaders who, having championed monumentally good causes, may eventually succumb to the delusion that their moral capital justifies decidedly unethical manoeuvres. Like the shoppers, such leaders believe that the greatness of their past deeds entitles them to a license for their transgressions.

Self-licensing paradoxes are common among corporations. We frequently see corporations vocally advocating for high-profile social or environmental causes, only to face accusations of severe ethical breaches in other, less visible, areas. Amazon is one example. In a report by Wenxuan Yu, Abeer Hassan, and Mahalaxmi Adhikariparajuli on Amazon's Corporate Social Responsibility, the authors concluded that Amazon performed 'very well in terms of social responsibility and sustainable development', particularly regarding climate change, environmental impact, and carbon emissions. Yet the authors also noted 'some shortages in terms of human rights, such as insufficient protection and care for employees during the COVID-19 pandemic, and labour union issues'.

Due to heightened scrutiny fueled by social media and rapid access to information, consumers are increasingly quick to see through such contradictions. Critics often label the companies' contradictory behaviours as cynical greenwashing or tokenistic marketing. In an era where every ethical lapse is instantly trackable, why do corporations like Amazon persist in a 'performative' corporate social responsibility strategy that so clearly invites public backlash? The licensing effect may explain their irrational behaviour; perhaps corporate executives feel entitled to the moral credit that accompanies high-visibility social responsibility efforts? Are they, just like the shoppers, rationalising their ethical lapses as a well-deserved 'moral break'?

There is no magic potion to immunise us against licensing bias. Mitigating its influence requires us to confront a difficult truth: we are rarely as consistently principled as we imagine ourselves to be. Resisting the self-licensing paradox requires resisting the urge to trade past virtue for present indulgence.

6
Smokescreens of Superfoods

While it may seem unlikely, the kitchen larder and fridge reveal much of our cognitive processes. That is because we rarely choose foods to satisfy hunger; the food we serve on our plates reflects our cultural background, values, and inherited beliefs. Consequently, the food we stock at home reflects our fears, opinions, and obsessions over our food choices. In reality, our dietary preferences are shaped less by scientific fact than by upbringing and the pull of social trends. When we shop, we often bypass the nutritional information on labels in favour of 'superfood' claims and influencers' endorsements; at the supermarket or farmer's market, we seek, more often than we realise, emotional reassurance. Food companies, keenly aware of this, have mastered the art of constructing narratives that tap into our anxieties and fixations.

To discover how easily our biases can complicate and concretise unfounded narratives about a particular food or ingredient, we only need to look at the enduring myth of monosodium glutamate (MSG). MSG is the original food villain. Wariness of MSG existed before the age of social-influencer-fueled food trends, in which social media is abounded with pseudo-scientific wellness warnings about 'toxic foods'. The ingredient was first identified in 1908 by Japanese chemist Kikunae Ikeda as the source of a distinct savoury taste. Ikeda developed a method for its mass production, and it has since become the key flavour enhancer used worldwide to add depth and umami to foods. But up until the 1990s, MSG was regarded as harmful because of a persisting, though unfounded, stigma. *BBC* highlighted in its article 'Chinese Restaurant Syndrome – what is it, and is it racist?' that it was a letter to the *New England Journal of Medicine* in 1968, in which the sender described having vague symptoms after a Chinese meal, that sparked widespread panic over MSG. Although the letter is now debunked as a hoax and scientists have discredited the myth since the 1970s, confirming that there was no clinical basis for the alleged symptoms, the term 'Chinese Restaurant Syndrome' and the misconceptions about MSG have persisted.

Nowadays, many news sources, including the BBC's article, culinary professionals, and historians, agree that the 'MSG hoax' was less about actual health concerns than xenophobia and cultural mistrust. The abovementioned BBC article suggests that the term 'Chinese Restaurant Syndrome' likely escalated because, when vague and unfounded claims about MSG's harmful effects were first publicised, the ingredient was widely associated with Chinese cuisine. The term 'Chinese Restaurant Syndrome', which implicitly singles out Chinese restaurants as the primary source of MSG, is clearly biased, since ingredients such as tomatoes, mushrooms, and cheese all naturally contain glutamates. Many processed foods, such as Campbell's soups, Pringles, and Doritos, also use MSG as a flavour enhancer; yet it was Chinese cuisine alone that bore the brunt of the MSG hoax.

Scapegoating Chinese food and restaurants was largely driven by negativity bias. Negativity bias causes us to give disproportionate weight to alarming information, thereby allowing fear to override evidence-based facts. Consumers' negativity bias may explain why, even after scientific reviews have repeatedly debunked the MSG myth, negative perceptions of MSG and Chinese food persist in Western nations. Out of necessity for business continuity, Asian restaurants in the US began widely displaying 'No MSG' signs to placate customers' fears and counter the ill-reputation of 'Chinese Restaurant Syndrome'. Chinese restaurateurs' decision to remove MSG as an ingredient in their menu was, unfortunately, a performative compliance with a largely fabricated, xenophobic narrative.

In the 21ˢᵗ Century, palm oil became a pariah ingredient in supermarket food aisles. Once a neutral fat, palm oil was quickly demonised as a health risk, even though the real issue was corporate malfeasance in palm oil cultivation. To capitalise on the demand for palm oil, unsustainable production methods were deliberately adopted, resulting in deforestation and the destruction of natural habitats. Amid backlash against unsustainable cultivation methods, food producers began labelling their packaging 'No Palm Oil'. While there are legitimate environmental concerns associated with unsustainable palm oil production, the 'No Palm Oil' food label often conveys a false impression that palm oil is unhealthy.

The Palm Oil Alliance Europe explains that palm oil is not an unhealthy seed oil. In reality, it played a vital role in food safety by replacing unhealthy trans fats in many products. Palm oil contains very small amounts of trans fats, with less than 1 per cent. It is naturally stable and makes an excellent alternative to partially hydrogenated fats. Switching to palm oil contributed to the near-total disappearance of industrial trans fats in many Western processed food markets. The 'No Palm Oil' label failed to deliver the true message: the environmental damage caused by unsustainable cultivation practices in palm oil and, by extension, in all high-demand, commoditised ingredients. The 'No Palm Oil' labelling appeals to our simplification bias: as consumers, we are often seeking to avoid the next harmful ingredient, while also coveting the next superfood without ever discerning the impact of our consumption habits on the environment.

In recent years, due to the growing global wellness food trend, food producers have increasingly deployed savvy food labelling that uses words such as 'natural', 'pure', and 'detox'. These 'clean label' narratives can easily turn processed foods into shelf-space winners, even when they may be functionally identical or mediocre compared to their unbranded peers. Because we tend to respond to how a product makes us feel rather than to what it actually does, a cognitive bias known as the affect heuristic often leads us to overestimate a product's true benefits.

Then there is also the hyping-up of superfoods, aided by pseudo-health experts who are mostly social media influencers who often spout unsubstantiated health advice, contributing to the rapid commoditization of ingredients that yield health benefits. The hype surrounding superfoods often triggers exploitative supply chain practices that marginalise and impoverish the very growers who produce them. Superfoods like chia seeds, quinoa, avocados, and many exotic roots and berries, regarded as the holy grails of longevity-promoting food ingredients, have become highly sought-after pantry staples. The surge in demand for these ingredients leads to adverse environmental and social degradation. As explained by researcher Magrach in the *British Ecological Society* report, 'Much has been written about the impact of crops such as palm oil and their obvious effects on ecosystems. Yet superfoods, which we associate with sustainable production and traditional use, are starting to follow the same path due to their increase in demand.'

The report detailed the adverse environmental impacts, including water depletion (avocados, almonds), soil degradation (quinoa), and reduced biodiversity (acai), all resulting from the growing demand for superfoods. Researchers have noted that although local communities have cultivated these crops for millennia, their superfood status has transformed them into global commodities, leading to takeovers by large corporations that often prioritise short-term profit over long-term sustainability. The commoditisation of superfoods puts sustainable, and socially fair, local food-producing systems at risk. Our insatiable demand for superfoods also reduces crop diversity, potentially causing these crops to lose their supposed health properties or resilience to climate change. Ultimately, it is our biases that drive exploitation in food production: as consumers, we are enticed by companies that use clever marketing to appeal to our desire for optimal health, which leads to surging demand for superfoods and, in turn, to the commercialisation that exploits local producers and degrades our ecosystems.

This pattern of manufactured demand also repeats with another new moral virtue in healthy eating: protein-fortified foods. In industrialised nations, protein deficiency is rare, yet the market for protein-enriched foods continues to boom. As Bee Wilson noted *in The Guardian*, 'Protein mania: the rich world's new diet obsession', nearly every food producer is jumping onto this craze. Plain milk has to make way for its more attractive counterpart: protein-fortified milk. Supermarket shelves are stocked with protein bars, high-protein yoghurt, protein water, and a wide variety of protein-rich products. Such products exist because of our mania, incidentally, fueled by pseudo-scientific wellness experts. There is no scientific evidence that consumers in industrialised nations need more protein or protein-enriched foods—much of the success of the protein food trend rests directly on our biases. Because carbohydrates have been cast as the villain in modern wellness lore, protein has stepped in as the hero. The growing popularity of protein-enriched foods grants manufacturers a 'free pass' to market their products with a high-protein claim, while tucking other ingredients, such as sugar, behind those claim labels. This irony is most evident in the ingredient labels of the 'health-shop' protein bars; despite their virtuous branding, most are little more than sugar-rich confections.

On the other hand, sugar is one of the most overlooked ingredients. From bottled kombucha and smoothies to vitamin-enriched flavoured water, food producers have artfully shielded it from our scrutiny with assuring labels such as 'low fat', 'natural sweeteners', 'high protein', and 'probiotics'. Innocent Smoothies and Vitamin Water are classic examples of how sugary drinks, through savvy copywriting and smart packaging design, are perceived as healthy food choices.   Driven by the affect heuristic, our subconscious gravitates toward emotionally reassuring language and attractive design, effectively closing our eyes to the actual ingredients printed on the food packaging. This cognitive shortcut becomes a silent partner in the sugar cover-up, allowing food manufacturers to deploy tactics similar to the notorious 'tobacco playbook' in downplaying less healthy ingredients with impunity.

Ultimately, the smokescreens of supermarket aisles, targeted ads, and wellness feeds are meticulously engineered to bypass our logic. Our food choices are never purely rational. Our biases influence our reasons for demonising some ingredients but canonising others. Deciding what to eat is an emotionally charged ritual. As long as our biases remain unaddressed, food companies and influencers will continue to curate narratives that dictate what we put on our plates. To counter our biased views of foods and nutrition, we may want to pause our frantic search for food elixirs and enjoy food as a marvel of our earth and humanity.

Traditions and Myths of Appetite

The influence of cognitive bias is most visible when it manifests in outcomes, such as an individual falling prey to a conspiracy theory, a financial scam, or a radical political stance. Yet we often overlook how biases infiltrate our everyday dietary habits—from the way we shop in supermarkets and prepare and consume meals to how we use food to define our cultural identity. This is because food is so embedded in our daily existence that our dietary choices rarely register as formal decisions; they feel like instincts. We don't perceive the supermarket aisle or our kitchen as a place where complex thinking occurs. Most of our food choices are intertwined with personal memories and cultural conditioning; our decisions often bypass conscious scrutiny because they seem intuitive.

However, our biases around food are clearly evident in our reflexive indignation at changes to a traditional recipe. At times, such as in the case of Alberto Grandi's theory about the origin of the Carbonara dish, indignation may arise from narratives that don't align with our beliefs or our knowledge of culinary traditions. Despite Grandi's plausible explanation of Carbonara's true origins, his findings were not well received by many Italians who adhere to the tale that Carbonara was an Italian dish invented by shepherds in Rome or by charcoal workers, the carbonari. Above all, Grandi's theory robbed Italy of its pride and culture. Their passionate reactions may seem exaggerated to any academic, but they point to an important observation about how we often behold culinary traditions with a near-sacred regard.

Across the world, food traditions, such as the elaborate Japanese tea ceremony or the communal feast of Eid al-Fitr, are not merely customs but fundamental aspects of identity. Ensuring the cultural continuity of these rituals requires practitioners to preserve collective memory and pass on the practices across generations. The very act of preserving a culture may lead to a protective mindset. Thus, any narrative or action that challenges deeply held traditions or beliefs evokes a strong defence mechanism. This is because community members may perceive counter-narratives as threats to culture, identity, and established preferences. As a result, a defensive mindset, fear, and other emotions often coalesce into heated resistance to any narrative that threatens our familiarity with our culinary traditions.

Food is also a reflection of our social status, virtues, ethos, and, sometimes, even our political stance. Our food choices are often subtly shaped by social contexts. Food trends, such as the consumption of 'organic foods' and the adoption of 'farm-to-table' practices, though initially motivated by a desire for positive environmental and health impacts, often conflate an elitist status with those who espouse such habits. Such is the case with the trend of grocery shopping with a fabric tote bag. The fabric tote bag, first popularised by designer Anya Hindmarch's 'I am not a plastic bag' fashion campaign, has become a symbol of conscious consumerism. This seemingly virtuous act of reducing single-use plastic bags, as research from Harvard has discovered, also emboldened tote-bag grocery shoppers' sense of entitlement. Their stealthy indulgence in less-healthy snacks is a phenomenon known as moral licensing, in which do-gooders unconsciously permit themselves to commit a less virtuous act.

Growing attention to health and nutrition has fueled a surge in wellness influencers, who now wield significant power in shaping public perception of food through unsubstantiated claims and simplistic, binary arguments. Wellness influencers frequently collaborate with food and health supplements producers to capitalise on consumers' cognitive shortcuts. Consumers' attention to food and its impact on their health began to emerge in the late 1970s, marked by a dramatic shift in lifestyle, one that was increasingly sedentary and characterised by a disproportionate consumption of fast food. That shift is attributed to rising obesity, and since then, consumers have become increasingly vigilant about their diets. That outcome catalysed sophisticated marketing strategies in the food industry that deploy a playbook tactic to both demonise and canonise ingredients and diets simultaneously.

Our digital ecosystem is an effective medium for the food industry's 'tobacco playbook' tactics. While we are fed with misinformation spread by pseudo-health experts, we also have access to exposés on stealth marketing tactics used by food companies. We are unfortunately caught in a confusing flow of information that sets us on an endless chase for the next 'holy grail' diet or ingredient.

All three preceding essays—the passionate defence of Carbonara, the secret indulgence of fabric tote-bag users, and our obsession with health food—illustrate how our biases shape our relationships with food. Whether it is the fierce protection of a recipe, the moral licensing of a conscious consumer, or the pursuit of a 'superfood' holy grail, these narratives reveal that our relationship with food is governed far more by unconscious biases than by logic.

7

SPH Media's Number Game

The print media industry was one of the sectors most severely disrupted by the digital age. Globally, print media companies face an existential crisis as social media platforms increasingly serve as primary conduits of information. Naturally, the shift to online news consumption has led to a sharp decline in print circulation and advertising revenue, forcing publications worldwide to adapt their business models rapidly. Many, such as Condé Nast, responded by restructuring and diversifying revenue streams through digital subscriptions and organising sponsored live events. However, Singapore Press Holdings (SPH) took a unique path: it restructured its struggling media business (SPH Media) into a not-for-profit entity. Its rationale was to free the media business from stringent shareholder expectations, allowing it to focus on quality journalism, invest in digital capabilities, and seek both government funding and public donations. Shortly after this major structural shift, an internal audit of the newly formed not-for-profit SPH Media in 2023 uncovered questionable practices. The company was found to have overstated its newspaper circulation numbers by about 10 per cent. The audit also discovered that approximately 82,600 daily copies were reported as circulated but had not actually been distributed. Some printed copies were reportedly discarded, stockpiled, or redirected to halfway houses in anticipation of audit checks. Others were printed under 'questionable arrangements', referred to as the 'X Barter Deal' and the 'Y Deal'.

SPH Media asserted there was no material impact on its financial statements. Falsifying circulation numbers is unfortunately prevalent in the publishing industry because circulation figures directly influence advertising rates and market perception. The review concluded that SPH Media ought to improve its internal processes and risk management. Nonetheless, the board and senior leadership were not implicated in any malpractices. However, one question remains regarding the inflated newspaper circulation figures: What compels an entire division to carry out and sustain such a cover-up of a plan that is recognisably unethical? Sustaining such practices would have required a concerted effort within the organisation. Could it reflect deeper organisational dysfunction? In the absence of direct accounts, we can only infer what could have enabled such practices at an institutional scale.

The absence of a whistleblower suggests that the work environment at SPH Media lacked psychological safety. Individuals likely could not question orders, challenge assumptions, or admit mistakes out of fear of retaliation. In organisational cultures where the fear of repercussions outweighs ethical considerations, employees quickly learn to keep their heads down and conform to established practices, even if those practices are questionable. Over time, a lack of psychological safety in the workplace can pave the way for the normalisation of deviance, a term coined by sociologist Diane Vaughan to describe how unethical or risky behaviour becomes acceptable when it goes unpunished or even rewarded. Once unethical behaviours become routine, whistleblowing feels more like a betrayal of the 'norm' and no longer a moral imperative.

Besides that, individual biases may also contribute to the questionable practice of inflating circulation numbers. Often, in large or bureaucratic organisations, work processes are siloed, information is compartmentalised, and individual agency is diminished or even eradicated, resulting in a diffusion of responsibility. In such a work culture, no one feels fully responsible; workers are more likely to rationalise their inaction and remain bystanders. In hierarchical environments, employees may be more inclined to defer to authority, reinforcing compliance even when practices are controversial. This combination of diffusion of responsibility and an inclination to yield to authoritarian figures may encourage groupthink. Groupthink is a psychological tendency in which the desire for conformity and harmony within a group leads to irrational or dysfunctional decision-making, suppressing individual critical thought and dissenting opinions. In the case of SPH Media, the combination of these biases may have allowed the inflation of publication figures to persist.

The questionable practice may also have originated with industry veterans who had sufficient authority to ensure its execution. If that were true, were those industry old hands led astray by loss aversion, fearing the immediate pain of declining metrics more than the long-term risk of deception? Or did the sunk cost fallacy lead them to double down on protecting the print-media legacy they had spent their careers building, rendering them unable to pivot even as the global industry shifted its gaze toward diversification?

We may never fully know the individual rationales behind the team's decision to inflate circulation numbers. Still, we can look to the Stanford Prison Experiment to understand how institutional roles erode individual ethics. In that study, participants engaged in ethically compromised behaviours simply because they felt those actions were demanded by the system they were placed in. We must question whether SPH Media's hierarchy fostered a similar environment where employees lacked the psychological safety to oppose the deceptive operative. SPH Media decision-makers are perhaps trapped by their own sunk costs. Their 'head-in-the-sand' response to declining readership left an ethical vacuum. Employees may come to rationalise their compliance as a form of obedience.

Much like the Stanford participants, SPH Media employees may have felt that protecting the company's perceived health was their primary duty, even if it meant compromising SPH Media's credibility as an upholder of quality journalism. The scandal is an illustration of the corrosive nature of biases on institutional integrity and ethics.

8
Anti-Social Anchors in Urban Planning

In a recent *The New York Times* opinion piece, 'Sports Stadiums Are Monuments to the Poverty of Our Ambitions', Binyamin Appelbaum offers a sober critique of the limited imagination of municipal leaders in the United States. He observes how it has become far easier for a city to greenlight the construction of sports stadiums than to approve housing projects. According to Binyamin Appelbaum, this stems from policymakers' fixation on large commercial projects, which they believe can act as economic anchors for broader development, including housing. In urban planning, these projects are typically considered 'fiscal anchors' because high-yield margins are expected to sustain economic activity, such as jobs, tourism, and tax revenue, for the city. Such a rationale has driven a trend of integrating stadiums with adjacent mixed-use districts to create cities as year-round destinations.

However, Appelbaum argues that such a mindset prioritises projects solely on the promise of high-yield margins while ignoring their actual impact. Academic studies have consistently concluded that public spending on stadiums is a poor investment; these developments have little to no tangible net economic impact on host communities. Although public subsidies often cover much of the cost, the primary beneficiaries are typically sports team owners and private developers. Furthermore, fiscal-anchor urban projects are catalysts for gentrification, which often price out existing low-income residents and local neighbourhood businesses. Despite these realities, municipalities continue to approve and subsidise these developments. According to Appelbaum, this lopsided priority reflects a failure of political will and a lack of creativity in reimagining urban planning strategies that could yield true long-term socio-economic benefits. He posits that policymakers and municipal governments must strive for solutions that provide diverse and, most importantly, affordable amenities such as housing and public transport, the bedrock of a city's long-term 'health and wealth'. Given that urban spaces significantly impact residents' physical and mental well-being, as well as social behaviour, Appelbaum is right to argue that governments must look beyond profit margins and prioritise investing in human-centric infrastructure.

In *The Architecture of Happiness*, Alain de Botton asserts that architecture inspires our emotions and can render vivid to us who we might ideally be. In the book, he expressed a visceral disgust at the harsh lighting and uninspiring atmosphere of a McDonald's in London, viewing it as a symptom of a design philosophy that ignores the human spirit. From my own travel experiences, I have been to countless public spaces that are merely reduced to commercially driven environments, largely soulless shopping malls dominated by formulaic chain stores. In those instances, my feelings echoed de Botton's sentiment. I often wondered: How does unimaginative urban design affect our state of mind, especially that of local youth? What is the psychological toll of these commercially driven environments on economically marginalised youth, whose daily lives are confined to uninspiring urban grids with little access to the psychological relief of open, public greenery and social interaction?

While fiscal pragmatism is touted as a tool for economic success, its misapplication often overlooks human-centric objectives. Relying solely on what 'works' commercially is a hollow strategy; true pragmatism recognises that an urban plan is only effective if it sustains the social fabric. The standard business model for major mixed-use developments often triggers a cycle of gentrification and displacement, suggesting that a narrow focus on invigorating economic activity is less fiscally sustainable than we assume. For global hubs like Paris, which rely on its unique cultural identity for tourism, an uncritical faith in 'fiscal anchors' urban development would be economically damaging. Parisian officials recognise the destructive nature of gentrification and actively resist such a narrow view of urban planning.

According to *The New York Times*, Parisian policymakers understand the necessity of managing the tension between market forces and social preservation; they view the protection of this balance, rather than the pursuit of big-ticket commercial projects, as the key to preserving the 'soul' that makes Paris valuable to developers in the first place. Through ambitious policy decisions, the city has invested billions into public housing to ensure that a quarter of its residents remain lower-income Parisians. They have even stepped into the role of landlord, directly shaping the retail landscape by prioritising small, independent shops over large chains to maintain a 'village' feel. Consequently, in any Parisian *quartier*, one can still find multi-generational bookstores, bakeries, and florists because the city ensures these business owners can afford to live where they work. Ultimately, Paris demonstrates that a commitment to *mixité sociale* is not only feasible but also economically viable, and that preserving social equity in urban development can underpin long-term fiscal strength.

Not far from Paris, Milan, Europe's other fashion capital, is facing a rapid exodus of its younger population due to the failure to manage the tension between market and social needs in urban planning. Milan's drain of talent and energy threatens to diminish the very character that has long made it a magnet for young professionals and companies. In Italy, regional authorities, rather than municipal governments, hold significant sway over urban planning and housing policies. Unlike Parisian elected officials, who have the municipal government's robust budget and explicit legal preemption rights, the Commune of Milan faces considerable difficulty implementing any decisive, large-scale urban planning. Milan's city administration often finds its hands tied when attempting to fund or approve public housing initiatives. The city has long been slow to approve new residential developments, leading to a chronic shortage of available homes. The influx of wealthy individuals migrating to Milan, driven by Italy's favourable tax policies on overseas wealth, exacerbates the housing shortage. Due to the high costs of land acquisition, developers turn even more aggressive in maximising their return on investment (ROI). In less than a decade, housing prices have risen, making homeownership unattainable for the average worker and young professional. While it is undeniable that the administrative conditions were stacked against Milanese policymakers, the city's trajectory serves as a cautionary tale, illustrating how a singular focus on fiscal gains in urban development can rapidly and systematically degrade social equity.

In land-scarce Singapore, fiscal pragmatism frequently trumps creative, community-focused solutions. In 2025, a plan to build an S\$1 billion wellness hub featuring thermal pools, saunas, steam baths, water slides, and extensive botanical gardens was announced. According to the news report, the development is targeted at a 'wide audience'. Given that it is a project helmed by the Singapore Tourism Board, I infer that the audience largely comprises tourists. According to the press, the development project aims to attract millions of international and regional visitors by creating a unique wellness destination. This is yet another example of how Singapore remains relentless in its focus on maximising land value and attracting high-yield development in its central area (locally known as 'prime district'). But there is a paradox to these remarkable big-ticket development projects. It is glaringly evident that the nation's savvy for high-yield development in its prime areas is losing its Midas touch. Orchard Road, Singapore's prime shopping belt, is now a three-kilometre stretch of commercial development featuring a monotonous, repetitive array of international brands and chain stores found in other leading shopping destinations.

Singapore's economic imperative and its very survival depend on attracting foreign direct investment, global talent, and high-spending tourists. Its continual drive for developing world-class infrastructure, sophisticated commercial hubs, and luxury retail experiences serves this objective. But such development spikes property prices, tilting the balance in favour of global brands and international chain stores. Many decades ago, the presence of global brands secured Singapore's competitive edge as a tourist destination. Orchard Road offered regional tourists a shopping experience that rivalled those of Western Europe. But Singapore's advantage as a retail destination is severely minimised amid Asia's upward mobility. New generations of wealth in neighbouring nations are more well-travelled. Global retail and fashion brands are also increasingly adopting direct-to-consumer models and establishing state-of-the-art boutiques in their cities of origin and in travel hubs worldwide. In this aspect, Singapore risks losing its unique position as a tourist shopping destination. Exorbitant land prices and commercial rents have effectively priced out independent, local retailers, creating a retail landscape dominated almost exclusively by international luxury conglomerates. The Singaporean shopping experience has become a carbon copy of the luxury boutiques found in Dubai or any cosmopolitan city. When a destination offers the same 'global luxury' found elsewhere, it loses its edge; well-travelled consumers have little incentive to visit places that lack a distinct local identity.

Unlike Singapore, Paris is known for both its luxury brand stores and its vibrant independent retail scene, and tourists are drawn to its authentic charm. For policymakers caught in challenging situations like those faced by Milan and Singapore, Paris has proven that its commitment to *mixité sociale,* in urban planning, one that sustains a resilient local economy and fosters deeper social stability, is as pragmatic as prioritising only economic outcomes, or perhaps even more. Paris's socially ambitious policies show that a city's strength lies not only in its financial success but also in its ability to sustain its residents. Parisian policymakers have proven that a city's greatness must not be measured just by its financial prowess or towering skyline. Insisting that every urban development project must justify itself with a guarantee of immediate financial returns limits imagination about how cities can be vibrant. With that perspective, fiscal pragmatism can become a trap, crowding out the small businesses, affordable housing, and local life that give cities their very unique character.

Growth-Fueled Biases

The term 'fiscal pragmatism' I used in the previous chapter is a derivative concept of the philosophical movement of pragmatism. Pragmatism holds that the merit of an idea or policy should be judged by its workability, usefulness, and practical consequences rather than by abstract or fixed principles. In government budgeting, this approach prioritises practical solutions over rigid ideology to drive growth, manage debt, and stimulate economic activity. While it is a rational and responsible framework, the workability of fiscal pragmatism depends entirely on decision-makers being informed by real-world experience, objective facts, and measurable past and present results.

However, in an increasingly complex world, this ideal is frequently undermined. Asymmetrical information and pervasive uncertainty make it nearly impossible to make perfect 'pragmatic' decisions. Furthermore, the drive for practical solutions is often hijacked by internal politics, intense competitive pressures, and the pressure to achieve immediate profitability to satisfy electors and shareholders. Most critically, because decision-makers are subject to their own cognitive biases, seemingly sound fiscal outcomes can carry damaging consequences.

As highlighted by pioneering economist Herman Daly in 'This Pioneering Economist Says Our Obsession With Growth Must End', an article published in *The New York Times*, growth has become the 'be-all and end-all of mainstream economic and political thinking'. The idea that rising GDP is essential for social stability and rising living standards has become an uncontested truth in modern society. But Daly, in the interview, asked critically: 'Does growth ever become uneconomic?' He argued that the current pursuit of rapid growth is causing such severe ecological harm that, counterintuitively, it incurs more costs than gains. Daly advocated for a 'steady-state economy' that acknowledges the physical limitations of our planet, seeks sustainable equilibrium, and challenges the growth idolatry of our present economic system. Daly's perspective suggests that governments, businesses, and even individuals who indirectly influence policies and business decisions ought to reassess a more balanced approach to fiscal pragmatism, one that also considers the well-being of society and long-term sustainability. The interview illuminates how our collective obsession with growth has warped the definition of fiscal pragmatism.

Transitioning to a model that prioritises societal well-being is inherently challenging because it demands a shift from the immediate to the intangible. Unlike financial returns, which offer clear and instant validation, the 'payoffs' of sustainability and social health are often realised over uncertain, decades-long timelines. When we operate within a system laser-focused on growth, our cognitive biases are often amplified. Our status quo bias deepens under pressure for quick wins. Under these conditions, it becomes psychologically painful to deviate from established metrics. Any alternative that offers intangible rewards is often dismissed as 'unrealistic'. This effectively traps us in a cycle where our emphasis on growth prevents us from imagining new solutions.

In the previous chapter on urban planning, we discussed how a singular focus on fiscal gains in urban development can rapidly and systematically degrade social equity. In Singapore, maximising land sales revenue is a critical source of funding for national development. But that approach has paradoxically led to Orchard Road, a prime district in the city centre, sacrificing its unique local character. This loss, as we have learned from Paris' mixité-sociale city planning policy, is plausibly exacerbated by high land prices that limit the retail presence of smaller enterprises. Due to past successes in using 'fiscal anchors' to maximise land's economic value, confirmation bias prevents Singapore's policymakers from pursuing bolder or more creative solutions. Due to loss aversion, policymakers fear losing economic competitiveness and potential land revenue. As a result, they are resistant to exploring alternative development paths that could be far more socially enriching.

The fixation on growth may also explain SPH Media's decision to inflate circulation figures. While the practice is ethically questionable, it yields immediate gains in attracting advertising revenue and sustaining shareholder confidence in an increasingly challenging media landscape. Amid the reality of declining print readership and relentless pressure to grow, SPH executives might have fallen prey to their own loss-aversion biases. Rather than confronting the potential loss of the company's position in the industry and their own executive roles, they preferred an unethical tactic to maintain a façade of financial viability. This pressure to avoid losses may have obscured the long-term consequences of their actions. The case of SPH Media illustrates how a ruthless adherence to growth-oriented strategies can compromise ethical standards and legal integrity.

Cognitive biases and the systemic prioritisation of growth reinforce each other in a self-perpetuating loop. An environment in which growth is the be-all and end-all of economic and political thinking fosters confirmation bias towards any solutions that have proven successful in generating growth in the past. Simultaneously, it fosters a mindset that strongly prefers avoiding losses to acquiring gains.

The success of Paris' *mixité-sociale* city planning policy was largely due to policymakers' courage in resisting this limiting fixation on growth: reframing their challenges and embracing the necessity to manage the tension between market forces and social preservation. Investing billions in public housing to preserve the 'soul' that makes Paris valuable to developers may not appear fiscally pragmatic, yet, quite the contrary, it aligns with the core tenets of pragmatism. Paris's success lies in its mixed socio-economic city-planning policy, which adapts strategies to real-world conditions rather than pursuing economic growth rigidly and superficially.

9
The Divine Oversight

The Industrial Revolution was a period of profound societal, economic, and technological change whose impacts continue to influence our modern world. It was also the tipping point at which the West's dominance accelerated, fundamentally reshaping global power dynamics. The Industrial Revolution began in the 18th century, with the transition of Great Britain's economy from agriculture to craft-based work and eventually to a manufacturing-dominated economy. That transformation spread across the Western Hemisphere during the 19th century.

One immediate consequence of the Industrial Revolution was significant environmental damage. As the *Digital Encyclopedia of European History* notes, Europe, in particular the city of London, became 'the cradle of the industrial pollution of the modern world'. The widespread adoption of coal for furnaces and steam engines contributed to 'dense smoke high in sulfur, hydrocarbons, bitumen, and heavy metals' saturating London, with fine particle levels comparable to those of contemporary Asian metropolises. The subsequent rise of the gas-lighting and chemical industries, particularly the manufacture of sulfuric acid and artificial soda, released corrosive gases and considerable volumes of hydrochloric acid between 1760 and 1800.

Other consequences of the Industrial Revolution extended far beyond the Western Hemisphere, most notably through the expansion of European colonial territories during what became known as the New Imperialism. Before the Industrial Revolution, colonising nations, which later became industrialised European powers, pursued wealth by maximising their nations' exports, minimising imports, and accumulating precious metals through state control and colonisation. That model of economic growth, also known as mercantilism, proved ill-suited to the demands of industrial production near the end of the 19th century. As the burgeoning factories of Great Britain and, later, continental Europe required an unprecedented supply of raw materials and new markets for their mass-produced goods, European powers intensified their exploitation of colonies, reframing their exploitation as an economic necessity. Much of today's global inequality stems from exploitation that occurred during the era known as the New Imperialism.

The decline of the Indian textile trade is a well-documented instance of the adverse impact of the Industrial Revolution and deliberate colonial policies. For centuries, India had been a major exporter of cotton goods, but by the mid-19th century, it was receiving one-fourth of all British cotton exports. That economic policy that made buying British goods a necessity wiped out India's own textile export markets. The British Empire also used legal and administrative means to seize land, transforming India's agrarian structure to serve its economic interests. The policy ensured India served Britain's economic needs.

But New Imperialism created extractive systems that could not last. While historians frequently attribute decolonisation to the exhaustion of European powers following the two World Wars, this narrative underemphasises the intertwined forces of colonial imperatives and nationalist resistance that had been brewing. India's economic devastation under British colonial rule was a direct catalyst for the 1857 Sepoy Mutiny, which sowed the seeds of organised nationalist movements; colonial exploitation created the resistance that would later dismantle it. As political scientists widely observe, the structural rigidity of authoritarian systems often prevents regimes from recognising their impending collapse. Besides institutional rigidity, long-held biases also blinded colonial leaders to their looming decline.

The ideological foundations of New Imperialism were built on biases laid centuries earlier. During the 15th century, the pioneering expeditions of Spain and Portugal were driven by both economic ambition and a genuine belief in a divine mandate to spread 'enlightenment' to a perceived 'unenlightened' world. This early religious justification established a precedent that framed the coloniser as a benevolent patriarch and their colonies as ordained subordinates. By the time of the Industrial Revolution, colonising nations conflated their technological and military advantages with an expanded sense of cultural, moral, and racial superiority, further fueling the belief that colonisation was not only justified but also a moral duty. This idea might have shaped a colonial worldview in which an 'equitable empire' was regarded as impossible and an oxymoron, further justifying increasingly exploitative practices.

Colonial decline was already occurring long before the two World Wars. This was evident in the late 19th-century decline of Portugal and Spain, driven in part by their rigid belief in divine mandate and a sense of moral superiority. Portugal, having pioneered the sea routes around Africa, established a global network of lucrative ports stretching from Brazil to Macau. However, by the late 19th century, Portugal was hollowed out by debt, neglected infrastructure, and internal instability. The 1890 British Ultimatum forced Portugal to relinquish its aspirations to a transcontinental African empire. Portugal's failure lay in overestimating the permanence of its historical prestige while underestimating the rising logistical costs of modern administration. These mistakes, in part, came from the belief that a divine mandate could sustain imperial control.

Along a similar trajectory, the Spanish state had regarded itself as the rightful bearer of divine global authority before succumbing to the 1898 Spanish-American War, which stripped it of its last major overseas territories—Cuba, Puerto Rico, and the Philippines. Spain's belief in its divine global authority made the Empire the primary pillar of its national identity. Thus, relinquishing a colony was equivalent to national humiliation. That ideological entanglement burdened Spain with the maintenance of unsustainable commitments to colonial territories that had become strategic liabilities. Portugal's and Spain's biased views of their rights and superiority prevented them from recognising the inherent weaknesses of their empires, which ultimately contributed to their decline.

Even Britain, arguably the most extensive and adaptable of the imperial powers, could not outmanoeuvre its entrenched biases. After World War I, the British Empire was both financially and politically stretched thin. India had become increasingly difficult to manage, as independence movements gained traction and moral legitimacy. The paternalistic British response, imposing harsher imperatives, only worsened its standing as a ruler. Britain's belief that its governance was not only more efficient but also a moral necessity for the 'advancement' of its colonies obscured the erosion of its legitimacy. World War II only hastened the empire's decline, which had already begun years earlier.

These missteps reflect a common bias among colonial powers: their belief in national exceptionalism. That same belief is observable in modern corporations and individuals. Companies have often fallen victim to the hubris of market dominance, with their biases manifesting as aggressive, unfocused expansion or a stubborn refusal to divest underperforming assets. The repressive top-down cultures found in toxic workplaces also mirror the moral superiority that justified colonial exploitation. When leaders see themselves as beyond criticism, dissent disappears, and mistakes multiply, obstructing any change needed for survival.

10

The Identity Rabbit Hole

In the summer of 2024, the Paris Olympics made headlines for marking a significant moment for queer and drag representation on a global stage. Along the banks of the Seine, Nicky Doll, Paloma, and Piche, contestants of *Drag Race France*, strutted along a runway. Together they brought a jolt of theatrical flair to a ceremony meant to celebrate unity and national pride. The crowd cheered, and many in the media called it a historic moment for LGBTQ+ visibility. However, the tableau vivant quickly drew controversy. Critics were quick to denounce the scene as blasphemous, citing its visual resemblance to Leonardo da Vinci's Last Supper. French bishops complained that the tableau scene was an excessive and provocative mockery of the Christian religion. Far-right politicians and conservative Christian groups quickly seized on the scene, framing it as further proof of what they saw as LGBTQ+ advocacy pushing anti-gender rhetoric.

Art historians in France and the Netherlands later explained that the tableau vivant scene was more likely to be inspired by a 17th-century Dutch painting of the Greek Olympian gods, *The Feast of the Gods*. Jan van Bijlert painted the work between 1635 and 1640. According to the Magnin Museum, where the painting is displayed, the similarities between van Bijlert's artwork and *The Last Supper* might have understandably confused viewers. The work was executed during the Reformation period, which might explain the artist's attempt to 'paint a Christ-related Last Supper under the cover of a mythological subject matter'. The creative director of the opening ceremony, Thomas Jolly, also confirmed that the tableau vivant was never intended to satirise Leonardo da Vinci's *Last Supper*, but was instead to depict 'a big pagan party linked to the gods of Olympus'. Jolly did not cite the exact painting that inspired the tableau, but his explanation aligned with art historians' views. After all, why wouldn't a tableau of actors depict Olympian Gods at the Olympics?

However, much of this reasoning was drowned out by the outcry over perceived blasphemy. To temper the fury and vitriol, the Paris 2024 Olympics organising committee apologised to Catholics and other Christian groups who had been offended by the scene. It was a measured and professional response, though it did little to quell the continuing backlash. It was as if the organisers' apologies were perceived as a tacit admission of guilt. Thus, unfortunately, the backlash continued through social media even after the opening ceremony event, escalating to the point of death threats against the organisers and performers. Thomas Jolly, ceremonies director Thierry Reboul, and Alexandre Billard of the events agency Ubi Bene filed a complaint for death threats. French DJ Barbara Butch, who performed in the sequence, also faced a torrent of online abuse. In a statement through her attorney, Butch shared on Instagram that she had been threatened with 'death, torture and rape', and had been targeted by 'antisemitic, homophobic, sexist and grossophobic insults'.

The backlash likely grew because conservative commentators amplified moral panic. Moral panic works by exploiting existing fears and prejudices to entrench a divisive 'us versus them' mentality. Gender identity and LGBTQ+ rights, particularly those of transgender individuals, have become the primary subjects of a burgeoning moral panic in public discourse. Although LGBTQ+ rights have long been politically contested, LGBTQ+ advocates have secured historic advances globally, successfully framing their rights as fundamental human guarantees. However, as the movement extends its advocacy toward gender identity and trans inclusion, the broad consensus often fractures. It is in this specific arena, where individual perceptions of gender are deeply intertwined with traditional biases, that the advocacy becomes most vulnerable to the trickeries of moral panic.

Vocal opponents of gender identity and transgender rights, knowing that fear can serve as a potent political catalyst, strategically exploit it to validate and reinforce the public's existing prejudices. They turn public unease into political leverage. To mobilise opposition against gender identity and transgender rights, they selectively amplify 'bogeyman' narratives. Such narratives warn of the danger and harm that will occur if gender identity rights are granted. A well-known example is the 'toilet debate', which relies on a fallacious warning of the danger to women and children when transgender women are permitted access to their bathrooms. Although the argument lacks empirical evidence, it excels at triggering fears.

The toilet debate taps into the broader, legitimate concern regarding the preservation of gender-segregated safe spaces for women, particularly in high-vulnerability settings like domestic violence shelters. The preservation of gender-segregated safe spaces is, on its face, a valid concern grounded in good intentions. Preserving gender-segregated safe spaces is also frequently championed by 'gender-critical' feminists like J.K. Rowling, who views it as a defence of sex-based rights. For that reason, she argued against granting transgender females access to women's bathrooms, citing her concern that by 'throwing the doors of bathrooms and changing rooms to any man who believes or feels he's a woman...then you open the door to any and all men who wish to come inside.' Ostensibly, Rowling presents her stance as a protective measure for women; it is indeed probable that aggressors may exploit the measure to invade safe spaces for women. However, how the argument has been framed is precisely where the case for gender-segregated safe spaces becomes muddled. Opponents of transgender rights opportunistically conflate two distinct issues: ensuring female safety and the unfounded assumption that transgender individuals are inherent perpetrators of harm, in their contorted warning against transgender inclusion in gender-segregated spaces.

In reality, the warning deceptively shields an established fact: transgender people are statistically far more likely to be victims of violence than perpetrators. By framing the expansion of transgender rights as an 'erasure' of safe spaces for women, opponents effectively turn the 'toilet debate' into a tool of cultural warfare. Rowling's passionate, if sometimes combative, stance provides anti-LGBTQ+ opportunists with an intellectual framework to advance divisive narratives.

However, the polarisation is not solely fueled by the opponents; a reactive rigidity within the LGBTQ+ community also exacerbates it. In their zeal to defend hard-won ground, advocates often adopt an uncompromising stance, treating any doubt as a direct assault rather than an opportunity for a civil dialogue. Framing the complex issue of expanding transgender rights as a choice between total inclusion and total exclusion risks alienating those in the middle and eroding any possibility of compromise. This is especially so in the field of sports.

The demand for absolute inclusion of transgender women athletes in women's sports often collides with the biological complexities that are highlighted by the scientific community. Arguments over the inclusion of transgender women athletes in women's sports frequently ignore the nuanced reality noted in scientific research. According to a 2023 joint statement by scientists, men typically outperform women in events relying on endurance, muscle strength, and power due to fundamental sex differences dictated by chromosomes and testosterone at puberty. Transgender women, assigned male at birth, may retain some of these advantages. While gender-affirming hormone therapy reduces these differences, some studies suggest they are not totally eliminated. For instance, a 2024 study published in the *British Journal of Sports Medicine* found that the absolute hand grip strength, considered an indicator of overall muscle strength, of participating trans athletes was lower than that of cisgender men but remained higher than that of cisgender women.

The transgender women who took part in these studies also showed advantages in parameters such as absolute maximum oxygen uptake and the fat-free mass index. In some respects, however, they performed worse than the cisgender women, for example, in the vertical jump with a lunge. While performance differences may be more pronounced in strength sports, such as weightlifting, they are notably less pronounced in sports like shooting or dance. The data shows that transgender athletic performance varies widely. These studies do not settle the question of the inclusion of transgender women athletes in cis-female categories. Instead, they highlight the need for further research and clearer, fairer rules. Rushing to frame any hesitance to allow trans-females to compete with cis-female athletes as discriminatory may overlook such genuine concerns and hinder thoughtful dialogues.

The complexity of including trans women in cis-female athletics is perhaps best exemplified by the nuanced, imperfect, nonetheless candid views expressed by Martina Navratilova in her interview with Kara Swisher. A lesbian and a fierce advocate for LGBTQ+ civil rights, Navratilova has nonetheless expressed significant concerns regarding the participation of trans women in women's sports, particularly where biological factors heavily influence performance. Drawing on her own experience, including playing against and even being coached by Renée Richards, one of the first trans women in professional tennis, Navratilova expressed her concern stemmed from her understanding that even after hormone therapy, male bodies often retain significant physical advantages in sports due to factors like bone density, lung capacity, and skeletal structure. While she firmly supports trans civil rights, Navratilova insists that her 'North Star' remains in ensuring fairness in competition, and thus her advocacy for segregation by biological sex in sports categories. She has suggested solutions such as a third, 'open' category to accommodate trans athletes, while openly admitting there's no perfect solution. In response to her anti-trans stance, Navratilova asserted that her advocacy is entirely separate from the cynical aims of right-wing politics, which 'don't give a damn about women' and are simply 'against trans people because they don't like them'. Whether we agree with Navratilova's stance on trans-women's participation in sports or not, we should view her concerns as a genuine invitation to find convivial and fair solutions within such a contentious arena.

In the film industry, LGBTQ+ advocates made significant strides with a notable increase in the representation of LGBTQ+ characters and stories. But at the same time, there is a growing debate arguing against casting straight actors in gay roles. Here once again, such a limiting rhetoric risks siphoning the LGBTQ+ movement into an identity swamp. An inflexible stance, such as opposing casting straight actors in gay roles, propagates a narrative of control rather than inclusion. The better argument is not who can play gay, but whether LGBTQ+ actors have fair access to a wider range of roles, not just roles that are tied to their actual sexual or gender identities.

Debates over gender identity and sports participation or the casting of gay roles in films have become deeply divisive. Our biased views, whether for or against, prevented an objective resolution. In part, our unyielding stances are driven by a moral superiority bias that turns complex issues into tests of moral purity and treats compromise as a betrayal of our principles. Thus, for those fighting for LGBTQ+ inclusion, they sometimes fall into the trap of perceiving the public's resistance to their causes as bigotry. For many non-political opponents of LGBTQ+ demands, resistance stems from a perceived moral encroachment, where the continued expansion of LGBTQ+ rights is viewed as an invasive overreach. Both perceptions are symptoms of a larger collapse in a centrist discourse. In the past, coalition-style politics required negotiation and a willingness to meet in the middle. Today, ideological fervour is favoured over genuine compromise; you're either fully aligned with a cause or you are an enemy. This entrenched divisiveness creates space for more extreme views, often harming the very people activism seeks to protect.

Activism that prioritises ideological purity over compromise often stalls the very movement it seeks to advance. The backlash against Diversity, Equity, and Inclusion (DEI) initiatives is another warning that framing multifaceted issues as absolute moral dichotomies can obstruct progress. When DEI implementation becomes a mandate, it risks being viewed by the public as an imposed ideology rather than a collective social benefit. Such a rigid approach creates an opportunity for opponents to rebrand DEI as reverse discrimination and an existential threat to established power and social dynamics. DEI is thus recast as a folk devil, readily weaponised for political mobilisation.

The fury surrounding these issues often reflects our own biases rather than the issues themselves. Without the courage to confront our own biases and prejudices, we will not be able to reach any constructive middle ground. The moment we stop acknowledging that our biases play a significant role in shaping our perceptions, we allow them to speak for us. When they do, even a joyful, harmless tableau vivant can be distorted into a vitriolic political firestorm. Yet finding this equilibrium is increasingly difficult in digital ecosystems designed to entrench us in our own moral high ground. These environments trap us in echo chambers that reinforce our prejudices. Unless we consciously recognise our biases and the cruelty that follows when we surrender our judgment to them, we remain prisoners of a narrow reality, oblivious to the forces shaping our thoughts.

11
The Moral Dilemma of Right Versus Right

In October 2023, the world reeled from the news of an unexpected and brutal attack that shattered the festive atmosphere of an Israeli music festival. Hamas and the Palestinian Islamic Jihad (PIJ) launched a devastating land, sea, and air assault from the Gaza Strip, resulting in more than 1,200 deaths, most of whom were Israeli citizens. The Economist described it as the deadliest day for Israel since the Holocaust. Besides deaths, more than 240 people were taken hostage during the attack. As the attack unfolded, graphic footage of the violence, including the abduction of festival attendees and the transport of victims, spread rapidly across social media, making the scale of the tragedy visible in real-time. The images and videos quickly sparked global outrage; Jewish communities in the US, France, and other countries held rallies in solidarity with Israel.

As Israel launched its counter-offensive, pro-Palestinian sentiment also surged across social media, mirrored by tens of thousands of protesters rallying across the Middle East, Europe, and the United States, all condemning Israel's strikes on Gaza. On social media, the historical and legal complexities of the conflict were frequently condensed into viral infographics and short-form videos. There was also a wave of graphic videos of wounded civilians in Gaza, most of which lacked verified data regarding when or where they were filmed. The content was meant to have a visceral emotional impact on viewers. Whether intentional or not, its lack of context also often obscured the tactical realities of the warfare in Gaza. Much of the social media content focuses on civilian casualties in Gaza while overlooking Hamas's military strategy. As documented by the NATO Strategic Communications Centre of Excellence, Hamas's military strategy involves using civilians as human shields to minimise military vulnerability and gain diplomatic leverage. By firing from densely populated areas or embedding military infrastructure within civilian zones, Hamas effectively increases civilian risk, complicating Israeli military operations. Equally important, human shielding serves as a military tactic to sway international perception of any attacks against them.

Regardless of Hamas' warfare tactics, the casualty data provided by the Gaza Ministry of Health, which the UN and other international bodies generally consider to be reliable, ascertained that Israel's counter-offensive caused an undeniably massive scale of devastation. In less than six months, close to 35,000 people, which included more than 14,500 children, had been killed, and most of Gaza's civilian infrastructure was wiped out. The International Court of Justice ruled that there was a plausible case for genocide. Israeli leaders vehemently insisted that the destruction of civilian infrastructure and the killing of civilians was never intentional; it was an unavoidable consequence of Hamas militants embedding within the civilian population, operating from civilian structures like hospitals and schools.

Hamas's alleged use of human shields remains a complex grey area. It is a subject that fuels much of the divisive public opinion about the war casualties in Gaza. According to a report from the Middle East Institute, while there have been cases of Hamas fighters and weapons located in or near civilian structures that violate international law, it is not always clear whether these were placed there deliberately as a war tactic. Gaza is among the most densely populated areas in the world, with some 2.3 million people packed into less than 140 square miles. Thus, there are very few areas that are not near civilians or critical public infrastructure. Both Human Rights Watch and Amnesty International have investigated similar allegations in previous wars and found no evidence of Hamas using human shields in the strict legal sense. Such ambiguities significantly contribute to the proliferation of conflicting narratives that are fueling observers' divisive opinions.

As mounting deaths of Palestinian civilians in the war zone were reported, a storm of polarised opinions, accusations, and ideological arguments intensified, further fracturing the public discourse. Public debate over the war soon split into opposing camps—sharply divided between those who asserted Israel's absolute right to defend its land and those who increasingly viewed the war as a consequence of Israel's harsh measures against Palestinian civilians and its aggressive settlement expansion in the West Bank and East Jerusalem. The rage surrounding the discourse makes it impossible for both sides to objectively address the worsening humanitarian crisis that has been exacerbated by Israel's large-scale ground incursion into Gaza since October 27, 2023. Worsening the schism is the Israeli government labelling its critics as pro-Hamas or antisemitic. Their framing strategically shut down any valid concerns over alleged humanitarian violations during the war.

The careless use of the phrase 'globalise the intifada' by some pro-Palestinian protesters inadvertently strengthens Israel's opportunistic use of antisemitism charges to shield itself from criticism. Pro-Palestinians protestors using the charged phrase lent unintended credence to Israel's simplistic accusation that all opposition to its incursion in Gaza is rooted in antisemitism. Individuals who used this term to express solidarity with Palestinians did not realise the phrase's historical reference, which connotes inciting violence against Jewish people, Israel, and its supporters. The Arabic word *intifada* translates to 'uprising' or 'shaking off'. It is most closely associated with two periods of intensely violent Palestinian protest and terrorist attacks against Israelis. The First Intifada, which occurred between 1987 and 1990, was marked by widespread protests, civil disobedience, and acts of violence, and the Second Intifada, in the period between 2000 and 2005, was characterised by widespread protests, demonstrations, and suicide bombings, resulting in high casualties on both sides. The phrase 'Globalise the Intifada' is thus perceived as a militant rallying cry to rise against Israel. Indeed, its indiscriminate use was attributed to inflaming lone actors around the world to commit violent acts against the Jewish institutions and individuals who show support for Israel.

Ultimately, this knot of divisiveness entangles both pro-Israeli and pro-Palestinian camps. As Nicholas Kristof noted in *The New York Times* op-ed, 'How to Think Through the Moral Tangle in Gaza', we often think of moral issues as involving conflicts between right and wrong. However, Kristof pointed out that the Israel-Gaza conflict is complex in consideration of the valid historical grievances and moral concerns on both sides; the Israel-Gaza conflict is a collision of right versus right. In his views, Israelis have built a remarkable economy and society and should have the right to raise their children without fear of terror attacks. But he also argued that Palestinians should enjoy the same freedoms and be able to raise their children safely in their own state. His op-ed perceptively argued that squishing a right-versus-right conflict into a zero-sum framework yields no pragmatic solutions.

The zero-sum thinking that dominates the Israel-Gaza conflict is a byproduct of our cognitive biases. Cognitive biases were also evidently the cause of the blundering response to Israeli filmmaker Yuval Abraham's award acceptance speech at the Berlinale Film Festival. Abraham won an award for his documentary 'No Other Land', which is about the destruction of a Palestinian community in the occupied West Bank. In his speech, he called for a ceasefire in Gaza and condemned the erasure of Palestinian villages. Paradoxically, German politicians and media outlets labelled the ceremony antisemitic and swiftly recast Abraham's humanitarian appeal as hate speech; German leaders were fearful that their silence would lead to the reassociation with the nation's horrific antisemitic past and also that Abraham's speech might unleash any unbecoming actions against Israel or the Jewish community. Ironically, it was Abraham who received death threats following his public criticism. Once again, a well-intended call for peace was distorted as an antisemitic threat.

Closer to home, Singapore-based blogger Michael Petraeus sparked a heated debate over the Israel-Gaza war. It all began with his criticism of former President Halimah Yacob's condemnation of Israel's actions as a 'continuing carnage'. Petraeus, writing under his blog *The Critical Spectator*, accused Yacob of hypocrisy; he specifically took issue with her comment 'keeping quiet makes us complicit'. Employing a classic whataboutism fallacy, he then suggested that her silence on crises in Sudan, Yemen, or Myanmar rendered her concerns for Gaza disingenuous. He also sardonically went on to label her 'complicit in the starvation of 3 million children in Sudan' as a retort to her comment that staying silent on the plight of Palestinians was complicity. Petraeus also asserted that Palestinian suffering was 'self-inflicted' due to the nation's support for Hamas, concluding that of all the war victims in the world, Palestinians deserve the least of anyone's attention. For a writer widely known for a 'no-holds-barred' objectivity, Petraeus's argument was inadequate, revealing clear bias. Even more dangerously, his argument appeared to insinuate that former President Yacob's stance was a biased one, perhaps because of her religious motivations as a Muslim. Petraeus effectively hijacked Yacob's humanitarian appeal and contentiously reframed it in religious terms.

The Israel-Gaza conflict reminds us that viewing this conflict as a zero-sum battle between two valid claims leads nowhere. When tragic events are reduced to ideologies and historical grievances, we not only lose the opportunity to unite around shared human values but also become oblivious to human suffering. Nicholas Kristof's op-ed suggests that the path to resisting this mental distortion requires us to hold multiple truths simultaneously, to acknowledge the profound harm on both sides, to grieve for the innocent without immediately politicising that grief, and to advocate for justice without vilifying those who frame the dilemma differently. To sit with conflicting ideas and emotions, we have to embrace intellectual humility and moral curiosity, which may help turn deeply fractious arguments into meaningful dialogue.

An Afternote

This essay was drafted in the immediate wake of the conflict; however, later events have significantly changed how the conflict is discussed. The early narrative was focused on the illegitimacy of the Hamas attack. Subsequent developments have increasingly shifted to questioning the legitimacy of Israel's operations in Gaza. Awareness alongside criticism of Israel's humanitarian violations has grown, as news reports suggest Israel's motivations include the potential displacement of Palestinians.

On August 8, 2025, the *BBC* reported that the Israeli government had approved a military takeover of Gaza City. With the announced objective to destroy Hamas and retrieve all remaining hostages, Prime Minister Benjamin Netanyahu had declared that his ultimate aim was the occupation of the whole of the Gaza Strip. The security cabinet wants the disarmament of Hamas, the return of all hostages, and the establishment of an alternative civilian administration.

Following this, Finance Minister Bezalel Smotrich announced plans to build 3,000 homes as part of the E1 project. Far from a coincidence, the E1 project is geographically pivotal: by building in the area between Jerusalem and Ma'ale Adumim, it effectively bisects the West Bank, severing the territorial contiguity essential for a future independent Palestinian state. Smotrich's own words that there would be 'nothing to recognise and no one to recognise' hint at a calculated effort to render a two-state solution physically impossible.

As these reports of territorial expansion merge with harrowing accounts of 'calculated starvation' in Gaza, the international community's moral anchors are beginning to shift. We are seeing a move toward a humanitarian perspective that is no longer held captive by Israel's accusation of its opponents as antisemitic. Even Germany relented and suspended arms exports to Israel for use in Gaza on August 8, 2025.

Also emerging from the conflict is the legal conundrum surrounding Palestine Action, a group founded in 2020 to end any global participation in Israel's settlement expansion in Gaza. The UK government's proscription of the group as a terrorist organisation and the subsequent arrest of individuals ranging from a 62-year-old woman in Belfast to King Charles III's former adviser show that we remain deeply enmeshed in a binary mindset. While the state employs a rigid legal definition based on Palestine Action's direct-action tactics, many supporters view their involvement in Palestine Action's protests through a humanitarian lens, driven by a desire to disrupt the machinery of war. This mismatch reflects how difficult it is to hold multiple truths at once.

Of Biases and Prejudice

I have chosen three seemingly unconnected developments for the preceding essays: the historical decline of colonial empires, the contemporary political divide over LGBTQ+ rights, and the devastating conflict in Israel and Gaza. While these issues occupy distinct temporal and geographic spaces, they share a common thread: they pose profound societal and political challenges that require a collaborative approach. In each case, collaboration is undermined by misaligned perspectives and ideologies. A major cause of this misalignment is the prevalence of zero-sum thinking, where progress for one group is perceived as an inherent loss for another. This adversarial mindset is often reinforced by deeply ingrained social biases around race, gender, and religion. They are biases that quietly shape how societies judge what is 'right' or 'natural'.

The origins of biases, about gender identity and social hierarchy, can be traced back to patriarchal agrarian norms and the historical influence of Christian Puritanism in Western civilisation. In agrarian societies, a rigid hierarchy served as a 'social anchor' for defining labour roles and social codes in a community. Such orders are also often framed as religious traditions or requirements. Because they transmit values and knowledge that foster social cohesion, community members who do not follow them may be perceived as destabilising. For this reason, social codes and traditions often exclude those who do not conform, limiting individual agency in favour of cohesion. Today, many of our social frameworks are still influenced by patriarchal agrarian norms and the legacy of moral absolutism.

Biases shaped by a rigid social and religious order manifest differently across the three situations mentioned in my preceding essays. For the colonialists, their staunch religious convictions provided the moral and philosophical justification for perceiving their occupation as a divinely ordained entitlement. That very bias also influenced a regime built upon oppression and dehumanisation. Such a regime is fundamentally unsustainable and subject to inevitable resistance. In the essay about LGBTQ+ advocacy for gender identity rights, opponents to the movement are often influenced by rigid social codes on gender and family, viewing any non-conformity as a threat to the established social order. Finally, the crisis in Israel and Gaza was also indelibly shaped by the legacy of Western colonial intervention. Once again, the allocation of territory for Jewish people in Palestine was based on a framework that was partly influenced by a longstanding Christian theological belief. Across all three cases, the inability to overcome inherited biases and zero-sum thinking prevents opposing parties from reaching for equitable, even if imperfect, solutions.

If we want a more cooperative society, we must first recognise these biases and their influences on our views. Political and social issues are far more complex than our binary mindset suggests, and relying on inherited cognitive shortcuts to make sense of what confronts us inevitably distorts reality. Greater awareness of our biases may prompt us to leave behind zero-sum thinking, a mindset that hinders collaboration, compromise, and the necessary actions to build a cohesive society.

Repercussions of Biases

Biases carry far-reaching repercussions. In this section, we examine how unacknowledged biases continue to produce measurable and often tragic consequences across institutions.

12

ExxonMobil's Foresight Trap

In 2015, the *Union of Concerned Scientists* published a report, 'The Climate Deception Dossiers', which suggested that corporations in the fossil fuel industry knew about the dangers of climate change and intentionally took steps to deny public perception of those dangers. The report supported these claims with internal company and trade association documents obtained through public records requests and investigations. Among the dossiers, an email from Lenny Bernstein, a chemical engineer and former in-house climate expert at ExxonMobil (formerly known as Exxon), revealed that the company was already factoring climate change into decisions about new fossil fuel extraction as early as the 1980s. His email suggested the firm was aware of climate change seven years before it entered public discourse.

In Bernstein's email, he shared a story about the company's evaluation of a gas field off Indonesia's coast. Bernstein, a 30-year industry veteran, wrote that ExxonMobil first became interested in climate change in 1981 while seeking to develop the Natuna gas field in Indonesia. It is a gas field with immense reserves, 70 per cent of which is carbon dioxide. That field would have been the largest single source of global warming pollution at the time. Bernstein's email implied that Exxon was aware of the link between fossil fuels and climate change, as well as the potential cost of carbon-cutting regulations that could hurt its bottom line. The company announced in 2017 that it would not continue the project due to high development costs.

ExxonMobil has consistently pushed back on suggestions that it knew about the dangers of climate change. The company has publicly stated that insinuating that 'Exxon knew' is a mischaracterisation. It argues that drawing a straight line between early scientific engagement and later corporate behaviour oversimplifies the complex relationship between the company's internal research, advocacy, and public policy. In its response to the *Union of Concerned Scientists'* report, ExxonMobil emphasised that it takes climate change seriously and believes that the environmental risks posed by rising greenhouse gas emissions warrant action. In the same statement, ExxonMobil also assured its shareholders that it is taking action to reduce greenhouse gas emissions from its operations, supporting research into technological breakthroughs, and participating in constructive dialogues with NGOs, industry, and policymakers.

Despite ExxonMobil's denial, a 2023 study published in *Science* repeated the claim made by the *Union of Concerned Scientists*. The new study reveals that ExxonMobil's scientists were uncannily accurate in their projections from the 1970s onward and that ExxonMobil's internal climate models predicted an upward trend in global temperatures and carbon dioxide emissions, as largely confirmed by studies on climate change. ExxonMobil scientists predicted that global temperatures would rise by about 0.2°C per decade due to the gas emissions from burning oil, coal, and other fossil fuels. The 2023 analysis, led by Geoffrey Supran and colleagues at Harvard University and the Potsdam Institute for Climate Impact Research, found that ExxonMobil's projections were consistent with and at least as accurate as independent academic and government models. The published study, which drew on over 100 internal documents, also found that ExxonMobil correctly rejected the idea that the world was headed for an imminent ice age, but instead predicted that the planet was facing a carbon dioxide induced super-interglacial. It added that ExxonMobil's scientists also discovered that global warming was human-caused and would be detectable around the year 2000. Despite its advanced knowledge of climate change, Geoffrey Supran claimed that ExxonMobil embarked on a lengthy campaign to downplay or discredit global warming. Rex Tillerson, then the chief executive of the oil company, maintained as late as 2013 that there were uncertainties about the impact of burning fossil fuels.

Given that my primary purpose of this book is to foster awareness of the subtle yet pervasive nature of biases, I encourage readers to resist interpreting the above-reported findings as conclusive proof of ExxonMobil's deliberate attempts to discredit climate change. For objectivity, let us also acknowledge ExxonMobil's claim of mischaracterisation and leave room for the benefit of the doubt regarding the corporation's true intentions. But that should not take our focus away from ExxonMobil's observed inaction on climate change, despite its knowledge and sophisticated, accurate climate predictions.

ExxonMobil's inaction on climate change was also implicated in a March 2015 article in *The Guardian* about the Rockefellers, descendants of the oil empire's founder, and their long, fruitless attempt to encourage ExxonMobil to change its stance on climate change. A detail reported in that article might hint at the bias that trapped ExxonMobil's C-suite executives. Rockefeller's great-grandchildren initiated an outreach effort in 2004 with a lunch meeting with ExxonMobil's then-head of investor relations. 'This was the family trying to get into a friendly conversation with ExxonMobil, feeling we have a strong historical connection with that company,' said Neva Rockefeller Goodwin, a co-director of the reform efforts. 'We wanted to start talking with the company about their views of the future and how they could be a constructive player as well as part of the problem.' According to Goodwin's recollection, the executives were startled by the concern. David Henry, then head of investor relations, was 'stunned' that the family did not 'love Exxon as it was'. Over the next few years, the Rockefellers launched three separate shareholder resolutions pressing the company to recognise climate change and invest in renewable energy. According to Goodwin, ExxonMobil executives expressed disbelief that the Rockefellers were not on their side on fossil fuels. They also dismissed the Rockefellers' suggestion of divesting from fossil fuels. Ken Cohen, ExxonMobil's former vice president for public and government affairs, called the Rockefellers' campaign out of step with reality.

The Rockefellers' account sheds an unflattering light on ExxonMobil executives' position on climate change. More significantly, it also raises a critical question about the executives' dismissive stance on fuel divestment: with ExxonMobil's technical talent, knowledge, and resources, why did it not view the Rockefellers' suggestion as a plausible step to redirect its capital toward renewable energy and climate solutions? (ExxonMobil officially established its Low Carbon Solutions business unit in 2021-2022 and invested over $10 billion in lower-emission technology since 2000. Its focus is toward investing in technologies like carbon capture and extracting hydrogen from natural gas, rather than traditional wind or solar clean energy.) Did their executives not see an opportunity to redefine their corporate footprint for the long term? Could biases have played a role in their strategic inaction, mirroring the institutional failures that famously crippled Kodak, BlackBerry, and Dell?

Organisations that once thrived under a profitable model often fall into three traps: inertia, sunk costs, and status quo bias. Executives often prefer predictability in business operations because it helps leaders make strategic decisions with greater confidence and minimises the potential for unexpected disruptions or negative outcomes. For a fossil fuel giant such as ExxonMobil, shifting course would have required not just foresight but the executives' will to disrupt the business system.

ExxonMobil executives allowed bias to harden into corporate inertia. In hindsight, the cost incurred is striking. ExxonMobil possessed the formidable intellectual and financial capital necessary to pioneer the clean energy sector long before the current surge in electric vehicles or the maturity of carbon markets. Instead of leveraging its vast resources to secure a foothold in these emerging fields, as the Rockefellers had urged, the company allowed its potential for innovation to be stifled by a preference for the familiar. This opportunity cost mirrors the slow-motion decline of other industry giants: Kodak, which patented the digital camera in 1975 only to suppress it to protect its film business; BlackBerry, which misjudged the touchscreen revolution; and Dell, which remained tethered to a direct-sales PC model while the consumer market evolved elsewhere.

ExxonMobil, Kodak, Dell, and BlackBerry are among the many stories of corporations that had enough knowledge to act but did not because of the debilitating power of human bias. Even today, when climate change is clearly a serious global issue, many world and business leaders continue to resist change due to deep-seated biases. The tragedy resulting from fossil fuel companies' delayed response is not only the environmental damage, but also our human fallibility in repeatedly failing to act despite recognising the threats.

13
Lingering Ghosts of Colonialism

In August 2025, the African Union, a continental group of 55 countries, endorsed a campaign urging organisations worldwide to replace the Mercator projection with alternatives, such as the 2018 Equal Earth projection. The Mercator map was created by the Flemish cartographer Gerardus Mercator in 1569. It was drafted to help European explorers navigate the seas more easily by keeping their compass bearings constant. But to achieve it, Mercator stretched landmasses toward the poles, distorting their true sizes; for example, Greenland appears about the same size as Africa, but Africa is actually about 14 times larger.

At first glance, we might dismiss this campaign as another wave of 'cartographic nationalism', given that this news followed the reported dispute over the geographical renaming of the Gulf of Mexico in the United States in early 2025. U.S. President Donald Trump signed Executive Order 14172 on January 20, 2025, directing U.S. federal agencies to refer to the Gulf of Mexico as the 'Gulf of America'. But what is interesting about the African Union campaign is its justification for replacing the Mercator projection: that the change is a step to improving everyone's perception of Africa. 'It is more than geography, it's really about dignity and pride,' said Fara Ndiaye, co-founder and deputy executive director of Speak Up Africa. 'Maps shape how we see the world, and also how power is perceived. So, by correcting the map, we also correct the global narrative about Africa.' Selma Malika Haddadi, the deputy chairwoman of the African Union's executive arm, added, 'It might seem to be just a map, but in reality, it is not.' The Mercator projection, she said, fosters a false impression that Africa is marginal, an impression that is subtly shaped by colonial bias. Changing the map is unlikely to address all the perceptions and biases about Africa, but it might spark a shift in thinking.

Whether the campaign succeeds or not, what matters is that the African Union has raised awareness of the Mercator projection's distorted portrayal of landmasses and that there are more reliable ways to map the world. Imagine that, with the new map, the UN and all government institutions and agencies had a more accurate perception of the African continent; they might frame their geopolitical relations with Africa a little differently. Insightfully, the campaign also reminded us that even a reliable scientific tool like the Mercator Projection carries inherent distortions. In this case, its widespread use perpetuates centuries of misrepresentation and a skewed global perception of the African continent.

The campaign to replace the Mercator projection brings to mind another narrative about Africa that needs a shift in thinking: waves of migration from Africa into Northwestern nations are often dismissed as a symptom of governance failure, which leads to fragile states, weak institutions, and internal strife on the African continent. Such a view conveniently overlooks the enduring legacy of colonialism. It ignores how centuries of extractive power dynamics have forged a lopsided global economy, leaving many African nations to cope with a political and economic reality that was rigged long before their modern institutions were born.

It is evident from the short-term measures adopted by Northwestern nations to ease migration, such as stricter border controls, that they do not view immigration as a multi-causal phenomenon. Governments often approach immigration with a defensive, 'not in my yard' mindset, treating the inflow of migrants as an external problem to be blocked rather than as a symptom of a systemic issue that requires a genuine and equitable partnership between nations. To this day, politicians have lacked imagination in addressing the complex root causes of migration. Border enforcement, which may subject migrants to inhumane conditions or push them into more dangerous situations, is still preferred because it is a politically simpler measure that yields greater visibility on governments' strict controls. For instance, in 2017 more than 6,400 refugees and migrants are stuck in Serbia amid winter as a result of Hungary shutting its borders; in June 2023, Malta was reported for delaying assistance to a migrant boat in distress for over 38 hours at sea; and Italy's government has been criticized for imposing regulations that force NGO rescue ships to travel long distances to effectively hinder its ability to conduct rescues in the Central Mediterranean Route, where most distress calls originate.

When immigration is framed mainly around issues in migrant's countries of origin (such as governance failures, conflict, and economic challenges) and the pressures on destination nations (such as economic strain, cultural integration, and security), an important reality is overlooked. Debates about migration often point to governance failures of migrants' countries of origin, which were once colonies. These debates rarely acknowledge the impact of the long history of exploitative trade relations. Especially in many African nations, it is an asymmetric relationship in which resources are extracted from them while their participation in more lucrative industries is blocked. Incidentally, this neocolonial approach, which institutionalised economic dependence and weak institutions, is one of the underlying causes of instability and corruption. Yet governments and corporations of Northwestern nations continue to cite instability and corruption as obstacles to investing in and improving trade relations in Africa. It is a self-perpetuating cycle that reinforces the power imbalance between Africa and the West.

Haddadi, the deputy chairwoman of the African Union's executive arm, is right to suggest that the global narrative about Africa needs to be corrected. In fact, the negative perception of

Africa and post-colonial nations, rooted in colonial-centric views, is a widely recognised issue that persists alongside climate, economic, and political challenges. In 2018, several news outlets, including NBC News and The Washington Post, reported that President Donald Trump allegedly referred to Haiti and African nations as 'shithole countries' during a meeting with a bipartisan group of senators at the White House. Even the leader of a wealthy, industrialised nation is not immune to such prejudice. Unfortunately, much of the economic and political instability in post-colonial nations has less to do with what these nations failed to achieve and more with how ingrained biases and a paternalistic worldview, driven largely by European nations during the colonial era, continue to create significant barriers to their self-determination and development.

A striking anecdote from Prince Harry's memoir, *Spare,* sheds light on this persistent colonial-centric mindset. In his memoir, Prince Harry detailed a 'territorial rivalry' with his brother, Prince William, over their charity work in Africa. Prince William claimed Africa was 'his thing' and questioned the need for both of them to run their charities there. In an article for *The Guardian*, journalist Nels Abbey commented that Prince Harry's account was shared with a great deal of obliviousness, leaving little doubt that, for both princes, Africa remains a colonial subject of their personal scramble.

One explanation for this persistent worldview towards Africa may be found in the 19th-century ideology of David Livingstone, who asserted that fighting the slave trade in Africa could be achieved through commerce, Christianity, and Civilisation. As a staunch abolitionist, he argued for the moral duty to extend British influence and development across Africa. According to Livingstone's idea, civilisation in Africa could only be achieved by combining Christianity with legitimate commerce to replace the Slave Trade. Unfortunately, that ideology was selectively interpreted and reframed to justify Europe's imperial ambitions, thereby facilitating the 'Scramble for Africa', a violent territorial seizure by European powers between 1881 and 1914, even though that was not Livingstone's original intention. Just as the Mercator Projection perpetuates centuries of misrepresentation of global geography, traces of Livingstone's complex legacy still influence the foreign policy, trade practices, and development programs of Western powers toward post-colonial nations.

Although the decolonisation of Africa was largely completed by 1980, imperialism never quite left the continent. The uncomfortably cruel story of *Opération Persil* illustrates how former colonial powers continued to wield dominance over post-colonised nations. *Opération Persil* was a covert French mission launched in 1960 to destabilise Guinea after its president, Ahmed Sékou Touré, rejected French economic influence and the CFA franc. The CFA franc, originally known as the 'franc of the French Colonies in Africa', was created in 1945 to enable France to maintain economic control following a post-WWII devaluation of its own currency. Using the CFA Franc was a condition of independence for many African nations. The condition was imposed to ensure that post-colonial states retain their foreign exchange reserves in the French Treasury, thereby tethering their economies to France. The French government did not tolerate Touré's pursuit of monetary and political sovereignty. French intelligence agency SDECE flooded the Guinean economy with counterfeit money and supported armed rebels, intending to cause hyperinflation and internal unrest. But the operations ultimately failed due to leaks and international awareness.

Today, the continued existence of the CFA franc provides a stable, low-inflation environment, but its structural constraints and colonial ties, increasingly seen as incompatible with the desire for full economic sovereignty in West and Central Africa, are yet another living proof of the persistence of a colonial-centric view of Africa. The currency, divided into two separate currency unions: the West African CFA franc (XOF) and the Central African CFA franc (XAF), is still used by 14 African nations. The West African CFA franc recently underwent reforms that included renaming it the Eco, abolishing the requirement that member countries deposit foreign-exchange reserves with the French Treasury, and removing France's representatives from its governing bodies. Nonetheless, the currency is still pegged to the Euro, and France guarantees its convertibility. This arrangement continues to prevent African nations from setting their own independent monetary policy to address economic shocks or promote growth. In contrast, the Central African CFA franc has not undergone these reforms, and nations are still required to deposit their foreign reserves in Paris, and the French presence on its central bank's board remains in place. While proponents of this arrangement maintain that nations benefit from the currency's stability, critics argue that it comes at the direct cost of monetary sovereignty and long-term economic development.

In contrast to France's imperial retreat, which was marked by overt violence, Britain's decolonisation is perceived to be a relatively fair and orderly transition. This impression is often bolstered by Britain's rhetoric of 'indirect rule' and the strategic implementation of a 'gradual handover' to its former colonies. Yet, the four-day conflict between India and Pakistan in May 2025 was a grim reminder of the Divide and Rule colonial strategy, used by the British during their reign over India. It was a tactic to keep the Indians divided, making them easier to control. Through Divide and Rule, religious and social divisions were institutionalised, which eventually led to the establishment of a separate electorate for Muslims, culminating in the hastily executed and poorly planned division between India and Pakistan in 1947. The resulting territorial dispute over Kashmir is a direct consequence of Britain's divisive legacy.

The extractive and exploitative nature of British rule was also evident in the systematic deindustrialisation of India, in which its once-thriving weaving industry was sacrificed to ensure the dominance of British textile manufacturers. The mass starvation caused by induced famines when food was taken from India to support Britain's war efforts was another exploitation, which many historians believe to be a contributing factor to the high rates of diabetes in the region today. Both the French and the British Empire demonstrated they were less prepared to grant colonised nations the freedom of self-rule. Instead, they were more adamant about protecting imperial interests during decolonisation and even after. According to a 2014 Stanford study comparing the British and French colonial legacies in Cameroon, both empires employed a similar tactic: withholding true agency until the colony was no longer strategically useful. The tactic was congruous with the systematic extraction of resources and people during the 'Scramble for Africa'. It is a mindset, rooted in a moral bias, that justifies the prioritisation of imperial gains. This same entrenched bias continues to perpetuate the unequal power dynamics between African nations and Northwestern powers, manifesting in trade and diplomatic frameworks that remain anchored in colonial-era attitudes.

In 2019, Ghana and Côte d'Ivoire suspended cocoa bean sales to demand a fair minimum price, citing unequal power dynamics. In recent developments, both countries boycotted the 2022 World Cocoa Foundation (WCF) meeting in Brussels to demand greater support for value-added production. Their continued push for industry reform seeks to dismantle the inequitable partnerships of the global cocoa trade. Demanding a fairer share of the value chain is a necessary step to combat the poverty and climate challenges in both source countries. Growing and harvesting cocoa remains the lowest-paid link in the value chain, with farmers receiving a mere 5 to 6 per cent of what a chocolate bar sells for in Paris, Chicago, or Tokyo. The cocoa trade still follows the pattern of exporting cheap raw materials to richer countries that manufacture valuable finished goods. Northwestern Power's monopoly over the lucrative chocolate-processing stage, while keeping source nations in the low-margin sector of the value chain, is a direct hangover from the colonial era.

There is no doubt that creating industrial capacity in chocolate production is exceedingly difficult in Ghana and Côte d'Ivoire. Outside large cities, reliable infrastructure like electricity, water, and sanitation is often lacking. Suppliers, skilled workers, and the necessary technology and equipment may not be readily available, and new start-ups may not initially produce enough volume to cover the high shipping costs. But these realities justify the two nations' demand for a more even-handed collaboration. The cocoa commodity business requires a significant share of labour and capital. As long as Ghana, Côte d'Ivoire, and other cocoa-producing nations remain at the lowest end of the value chain, they are less likely to diversify their economies or plan for long-term growth. However, through an equitable partnership, cocoa-producing nations such as Ghana and Côte d'Ivoire will have the opportunity to build the necessary infrastructure and a skilled workforce for chocolate production, thereby reducing their dependence on commodity exports.

While pragmatic concerns about Ghana's and Côte d'Ivoire's industrial readiness for chocolate production are well-justified, small enterprises like Fairafric, as reported by *The New York Times*, have succeeded in reversing the status quo by operating a chocolate factory directly in Amanase, Ghana. The success of a small producer who chose to invest locally calls into question the inertia of global giants with their vast resources. Could the lack of interest in addressing the entrenched barriers that prevent cocoa-producing nations from transitioning into manufacturing be not about market or business logic, but about preserving a status quo uniquely advantageous to multinational corporations with centuries of dominance in the trade? Are the challenging realities of establishing chocolate production convenient smokescreens that help perpetuate the imbalance in the partnership, placing cocoa-producing nations like Ghana and Côte d'Ivoire in a weaker position rather than as peers in the global enterprise? Are multinational corporations still adopting a colonial-centric bias that prevents them from considering African nations as equal partners?

What confronts European powers today is a vicious cycle perpetuated by the lingering ghosts of colonialism. Unfair trade rules and currency regimes undermine political and social stability in post-colonised Africa, reasons that compel Africans to migrate, often to Europe. These migrants became easy scapegoats for Europe's broader social problems. Their presence is often portrayed as that of folk devils within extreme political ideologies. But those narratives obscure the reality that the influx of migrants is a direct consequence of a colonial-centric mindset that continues to impose inequitable trade and political policies on Africa. In some ways, Europe inadvertently manufactures the very political volatility and social erosion. In this sense, Europe faces the political consequences of its inability to dismantle its colonial-centric world views.

14
Sins of Inhospitality

The first recognised alert about AIDS was issued on June 5, 1981. The U.S. Centres for Disease Control (CDC) published a report on a rare lung infection, *Pneumocystis carinii* pneumonia, in five young, previously healthy gay men in Los Angeles. A month later, the CDC issued another warning about a cluster of rare diseases affecting gay men in Los Angeles and New York. The *New York Times* headlined the finding 'Rare Cancer Seen in 41 Homosexuals'. Early news headlines often reinforced an incorrect perception that AIDS affected only gay men. That perception, in some measure, provoked moral judgment and homophobia, and delayed the health authorities' response. As a result, they failed to focus on the virus's modes of transmission, turning a medical crisis into a catastrophic failure of leadership.

While that narrow public perception of AIDS, that it only affected male homosexuals, was gaining ground, evidence of the disease in non-homosexuals was also emerging. In late 1981, a pediatric immunologist at Albert Einstein Medical College in New York was treating infants with severe immune deficiency whose mothers were drug users. He recognised a pattern similar to the immune deficiency affecting gay men, but his colleagues dismissed his diagnosis. In July 1982, the first cases of immunosuppression were reported in patients with haemophilia who had no other known risk factors. Despite all that mounting evidence that the epidemic affected not only gay men, the biased association of the disease with homosexual activity continued to influence the US authorities from taking adequate actions to contain its spread.

It was only in September 1982 that two House representatives from California and New York, states with communities affected by the epidemic, introduced the first legislation to allocate funding for AIDS research. But the Congress did not approve the funding. Persistent stigma of AIDS and the Reagan administration's overall agenda to cut federal budgets prevented what would have been the first dedicated funding for AIDS research and treatment. Funding was only approved in July 1983, two years after the epidemic was declared. In addition to the delayed response, critics of the Reagan administration also lambasted the severely insufficient funds. Randy Shilts, in his book *And the Band Played On,* wrote that the approved research funding for AIDS in 1983 and the preceding years was highly insufficient and blamed many institutions, including the government, for allowing the epidemic to spread much further and faster than necessary.

It was indeed a lack of public leadership during the early stages of the epidemic that contributed to a delayed, hesitant response. President Reagan did not publicly mention the disease until a press conference in September 1985, more than four years later. Larry Speakes, Reagan's White House Press Secretary, was notably evasive of reporters' questions on AIDS. On some occasions, he even responded with thinly veiled gay jokes at the expense of the reporters who asked. Even years later, public health officials' efforts to educate the public about the disease were constrained by the Helms Amendment of 1988. This law banned any federally funded materials deemed to be promoting homosexual activity.

Much of the Reagan administration's inertia on affirmative action to curb the epidemic, whether through research, public education, and funding for the CDC, was due to an ideological moral bias, though unlikely to be the President's. President Ronald Reagan's views on homosexuality had been surprisingly liberal before he was elected. As the governor of California, he opposed the Briggs Initiative, a California ballot measure that would have banned gay people and their supporters from working in public schools. Having gay men among his close friends from his Hollywood days might have influenced his opposition. Yet, after winning the presidency with the overwhelming support of a newly mobilised conservative Christian base, the Reagan administration had to align its public image with the political priorities of the religious conservatives, who are its strongest backers. Many of the religious conservatives perceived AIDS as a consequence of moral failing. Thus, keeping a distance from the issue, to maintain support from that conservative base, was a politically expedient move by the Reagan administration. However, the hesitancy to take effective action or educate the public was not limited to the US; it was evident in many other countries. Due to AIDS's stigmatised association with gay men, leaders feared that taking any affirmative actions might imply their tolerance or acceptance of homosexuality, a social taboo that was and still is widely considered a 'sinful lifestyle'.

That homosexuality is immoral is a Christian religious narrative drawn from a particular interpretation of the biblical story of Sodom and Gomorrah. For centuries, Christian doctrine had cast homosexuality as a form of divine transgression. Many mainstream churches in the 1980s continued to view AIDS as 'divine retribution'. As historian Anthony Petro observed, even liberal Christian communities were slow to respond to the AIDS epidemic, with most issuing statements of compassion only well into the mid-to-late 1980s. Thousands had already died of AIDS by then.

Interestingly, there were alternative theological readings of Sodom and Gomorrah that might have changed the course of the AIDS epidemic had such readings become mainstream Christian narratives. Theologian Derrick Bailey and historian John Boswell offered a compelling alternative, both interpreting the story as a warning against inhospitality and cruelty instead of a condemnation of same-sex desire. The renowned artist and filmmaker Derek Jarman reportedly owned several copies of Boswell's study and frequently cited it in his writings in support of Boswell's thesis, which was derived from Bailey's works. Boswell reasoned that the biblical story of Sodom concerned the lack of hospitality. Jarman, who was diagnosed with HIV in 1986, argued that the true moral failing of the AIDS epidemic, in the context of Bailey's and Boswell's thesis, was not homosexuality; it was society's indifference to the plight of those who fell ill. 'If the sin of the people of Sodom was inhospitality,' he wrote in *At Your Own Risk: A Saint's Testament,* 'the lack of hospitality that we have received in my lifetime reveals a true Sodom in the institutions of my country.'

Derek Jarman's argument highlights the significant role that interpretations of religious texts play in shaping perceptions of morality and behaviour in religious institutions and societies. Had interpretations emphasised themes of grace, forgiveness, and universal love, the institutional response to the AIDS crisis could have been decidedly different. Instead of a response stifled by moral condemnation, it could be one with empathy, and that might have accelerated medical intervention and public support, preventing the thousands of unnecessary deaths of male homosexuals, who were essentially sanctioned as immoral. Unfortunately, as Jarman angrily lashed out in his writings, our social order and ethical norms are often constructs rooted in the agrarian and patriarchal ideologies of the past. These frameworks, designed to establish social order, undermined efforts to contain the AIDS epidemic. To this day, they continue to influence our rationale. In this light, our inherited moral frameworks hold sway over most of the decisions we take.

The response to the AIDS epidemic in the Asia Pacific region was vast and diverse. But one commonality was that the disease's impact was first observed among the marginalised community of male sex workers and intravenous drug users. The inadequate measures taken to combat the epidemic at its onset in the Asia Pacific were likely due to the region's relatively limited health services and expertise at the time. However, in view of the fact that the epidemic was also first discovered in the gay community there, another possible cause of this inadequacy is the stigma attached to homosexuality.

Many post-colonial nations' societal norms are heavily influenced by Christian doctrines introduced by European colonisers and missionaries. In 1862, British historian Lord Thomas Babington Macaulay drafted the Indian Penal Code, with the intention of 'protecting innocent British soldiers from the exotic, mystical Orient'. Then, there was a biased orientalised view of Asia and the Middle East that the inhabitants there were 'overly erotic'. The penal code, which contained section 377, ruled that 'whoever voluntarily has carnal intercourse against the order of nature with any man, woman or animal' would be punished with imprisonment or fines. It was a law modelled after Britain's 16th-century Buggery Act. LGBTQ+ activists have always argued that the Indian Penal Code, which contained section 377, is a damaging legacy against LGBTQ+ people. While Britain's law against sex with men was removed with the Sexual Offences Act 1967, many of its post-colonised nations continue to uphold Section 377. In some of these nations that once held flexible attitudes towards LGBTQ+ people before British colonial occupation, homosexuality became an act that warrants severe punishment under the law.

Britain's Section 377 legacy might be a plausible explanation of the curious case of Singapore's rather conservative approach to the AIDS epidemic, a nation often recognised for its secularity and pragmatism in policymaking. When HIV infections were discovered in Singapore, the government's reaction mirrored that of the Western world. There were clampdowns on gay gathering spaces, secrecy around deaths, and an unwillingness to talk openly about the epidemic. In a *Rice Media* retrospective article on AIDS in Singapore, a care worker recalled: 'It was all very hush-hush. People didn't want to talk about it. No one wanted to know who died of

AIDS.' One particularly tragic irony mentioned in the article is the experience of Freddie, a patient who discovered his infection through a routine blood donation, for which he was criminally charged with false disclosure. To this day, Singapore maintains a ban on blood donations from gay men, echoing the same moral attitude. It is yet another cautionary tale about how our cognitive biases can distort judgment and affect everything from individual attitude to institutional laws and policies. The biased views on AIDS drowned out compassionate and rational considerations that could have saved the generations lost.

Even today, bias, driven by conservative religious interpretations, over AIDS and HIV lingers. In 2025, the Trump administration announced it would cut funding for the President's Emergency Plan for AIDS Relief program. Ostensibly, the cut in funding was intended to end nations' reliance on American foreign aid and to shift responsibility to African nations and the private sector. However, conservative think tanks that campaigned for the cuts, such as The Heritage Foundation, argued that the move is well justified because HIV is a 'lifestyle disease' which could be prevented through education and abstinence. Their argument hints at moral bias and indirectly implies that people living with HIV could have avoided the disease through self-will and abstinence from 'risky sexual behaviours'. Even within the LGBTQ+ community itself, the same moral biases persist. Disagreements among gay men regarding Pre-exposure Prophylaxis, commonly known as PrEP, often stem from stigma and moral judgments. Although a breakthrough preventive medication, PrEP is sometimes unfairly cast as an enabler of promiscuity and irresponsibility rather than an efficacious drug that empowers individuals with greater agency over their sexual health.

The cost of bias surrounding AIDS and HIV has been existential. The AIDS epidemic has had a devastating, generation-altering impact globally, claiming over 35 to 40 million lives since the early 1980s. AIDS killed a significant portion of the working-age population in many African nations, leaving behind millions of orphans. The scale of this loss was akin to the toll of wars. It was an unnecessary loss. Had history heeded alternative theological interpretations of Sodom and Gomorrah, had compassion, rather than condemnation, guided leaders' response to the epidemic, the narrative we inherit today of the AIDS epidemic might look fundamentally different. Instead, we witness how a dominant moral bias, that framed homosexuality as a sin and the AIDS crisis as its divine retribution, distorted perception, dictated policies, delayed medical intervention, and ultimately decided who was worthy of care and who was left to die.

15
A Price Tag on Ethics

In September 2024, protests erupted outside Montblanc's flagship store in Geneva. The protesters, flanked by union officials from Italy and Switzerland, accused the pen and watchmaker of dropping its supplier, Z Production, last year after unions helped Z Production's workers secure compensation payments and improved workplace safety.

According to a report by *Public Eye*, Z Production was subjecting workers to unlawful working conditions. In an interview with one of the workers, Muhammad Arslan, he revealed, 'We had to work until eight o'clock in the evening, twelve hours a day, with just a half-hour break. And six days a week instead of 5. We couldn't take any holidays either.' It seemed that conditions might improve when the workers sought assistance from a local trade union, Sudd Cobas. By intensifying their organised protests, employees such as Arslan finally secured a new agreement with Z Production on February 9, 2023. The agreed changes guaranteed workers would no longer be required to work more than the legal maximum hours. They would also be entitled to their holidays and sick leave.

Before the agreed-upon improvements could take effect, Z Production announced layoffs of all its workers shortly after. It claimed that its sole client, Pelletteria Richemont, had slashed production volumes and that on February 28, they decided to terminate the contract by the end of 2023. Pelletteria Richemont (Richemont Leather Goods) is a direct subsidiary of the Compagnie Financière Richemont group. This major luxury conglomerate owns the Montblanc brand. Pelletteria Richemont manages the production of Richemont Group's leather goods in Italy. Richemont confirmed the termination. According to Richemont Group's response to *Public Eye*, the decision was reached after Z Production repeatedly failed to comply with Richemont's supplier code of conduct.

The protestors at Montblanc's flagship store in Geneva sought to raise awareness of the questionable timing of the layoffs and of Richemont's decision to terminate its contract with Z Production shortly after Sudd Cobas had established legal working conditions with the employees. The protestors argued that the labour dispute at Z Production began as early as 2019, insinuating that the termination of Z Production's contract in 2023 casts doubt on Richemont's explanation. In response to the protestors, Richemont stressed that February 2023 marked the breaking point after it discovered an undeclared subcontractor during an audit.

In an *Al Jazeera* documentary titled 'Inside Italy's designer bag sweatshops', journalists posed as investors to gain access to factories that produce leather bags for luxury brands. By chance, they uncovered a Chinese leather goods factory, Pelletteria A&S, located about five kilometres from the Z Production site in June 2024. In the video footage of the reportage, workers are seen without adequate safety precautions. The owner, who called herself Sofia, specifically stated that she had sacked her Bangladeshi workers after they filed complaints about working conditions at the factory. She added that she would only hire Chinese workers, who were more obedient and would never behave in such a manner. The Montblanc star logo was also clearly visible on some leather bags, further suggesting that the contract might have been transferred from Z Production to another company. *Al Jazeera* was unable to ascertain if its reported assumption was true.

In response to the protest in Geneva, Montblanc continued to stand by Richemont's explanation that Z Production's contract was terminated for failing to meet its supplier code of conduct. To further their stance, Montblanc also sued the three Sudd Cobas officials for defamation and coercion. In its statement to *Public Eye*, Richemont claims that 'these individuals in particular have and continue to wage a slander campaign against Montblanc, based on testimonies from a very small number of former workers who are using the termination of the business relation with Z Production as a means of damaging Montblanc's reputation in Italy and internationally'. For legal clarity, all of the aforementioned observations in this essay do not constitute proof of Richemont's alleged ethical lapse.

The labour dispute at Richemont is part of a broader, growing scrutiny of the Italian luxury-goods supply chain, in which luxury brands such as LVMH, Armani, and Kering have also faced investigations into alleged labour violations. Between January and June 2024, a Milan court placed Dior, Armani, and Alviero Martini under judicial administration due to the exposure of sweatshop-like conditions at 16 workshops that manufactured products for those brands. A year later, Loro Piana, part of LVMH, became the fifth high-end brand in Italy to be placed under judicial administration for culpably failing to oversee its suppliers' handling of worker abuses. In light of the judicial administration, Armani Group stated that it was surprised by the subcontractors' actions, which violated the group's core values, and has since implemented corrective organisational measures to resolve the issue. LVMH, the conglomerate that owns Loro Piana and Dior, stated in its announcement that it 'has been constantly reviewing and will continue to strengthen its control and audit activities' to ensure compliance with its own quality and ethical standards throughout the supply chain.

Richemont's response mirrors a familiar pattern among luxury brands facing allegations of labour violations: denying direct responsibility and often shifting the ethical breaches to suppliers. Due to the complex, opaque supply chains in the fashion industry, luxury brands may be unaware of labour violations. In support of the luxury brands' claims, industry figures such as Carlo Capasa, president of Italy's National Fashion Chamber, have also insisted that auditing 21,000 sub-suppliers is nearly impossible. However, it is also worth asking whether the fashion industry's opaque supply chains allow luxury brands to maintain plausible deniability about how their products are really made.

Capasa's reasoning overlooks how industry practices may have created that opacity in the first place, allowing brands to benefit from their own oblivion or neglect. Labour exploitation often emerges when brands demand unrealistically low production prices. One way for suppliers to sustain such exacting agreements is by exploiting sub-suppliers' workers. By leaning on the excuse that outsourcing supply chains was often complex and opaque, it would appear that companies are engaging in a form of moral abdication, deliberately distancing themselves from the ethical consequences of their supply chain practices.

In the film *Greed*, Steve Coogan's character, Sir Richard Macreadie, a retail chain mogul, insists he bore no direct responsibility for the fire that killed his assistant's mother, who was a worker in that very garment factory that manufactured clothing for his retail chain. In response to his claim, Amanda, his assistant, releases a lion from its cage in his presence. Her action led to Macreadie's death. But she, mirroring Macreadie's rationale, defended that it was the lion and not her who committed the killing, arguing that she merely 'pushed the button' that opened the cage and freed the lion. Macreadie's death, Amanda concluded, was a direct consequence of the lion's attack, not hers. Amanda's reasoning is a biting commentary on present-day practices in the fashion industry: the more removed companies are from the hands that stitch, dye, and assemble their goods, the easier it is to claim oblivion of any poor working conditions.

Fragmented supply chains allow brands to distance themselves from labour violations. Because using intermediaries keeps the production at arm's length, executives are assured of a physical and legal chasm that allows them to disavow any ethical lapses. Judging by the fervour of high-profile press events and social media engagement, labour violations have failed to dent consumers' aspirations; the desire for luxury brands remains remarkably resilient in the face of ethical scandals. This is because luxury brands' sophisticated marketing taps into consumer bias by presenting an illusion of heritage and integrity. In this dynamic, the consumer unknowingly supports a system of plausible deniability.

Exploiting consumers' biases to maintain plausible deniability is not limited to the luxury sector. In 2023, fast-fashion giant Shein, dogged by accusations of labour rights violations and environmental harm, invited a group of influencers on a curated junket to tour one of its 'model' factories in China. Shein aimed to dispel accusations that its suppliers are subjecting workers aged 23 to 60 to a 12-hour workday without meal breaks. The invited influencers dutifully posted glowing reviews of the facilities and passionately dismissed any online critics. How Shein chose to spend its money reveals how well companies understand the importance and effectiveness of leveraging humans' biases to curate messages to their advantage. Despite the backlash of the manipulative junket tour, Shein continues to flood the market with €10 dresses and €5 tops, price points that make ethical production almost mathematically impossible.

This persistent cycle of exploitation in the fashion industry is a manifestation of deeply ingrained human biases. The opaque, distant production facilities might serve a dual purpose: minimising operational costs while dehumanising the workers. This psychological distance makes it easier for executives to prioritise profit while remaining oblivious to the harsh reality of predatory working conditions and meagre wages. As consumers, we tend to separate our consumption from ethical implications, allowing the immediate gratification of a luxury purchase or a fast-fashion bargain to override any ethical concerns. 'Ethical decoupling' allows us to indulge our wants while ignoring any systemic neglect that often underpins the production of fashion goods. In this way, both brands and consumers perpetuate the cycle of exploitation. Despite the recurring public outrage over ethical breaches, human biases continue to serve as a protective buffer, shielding the fashion industry from genuine reform. Unless we acknowledge and end both our active and passive involvement in this wrongdoing, the industry will continue to rely on exploited labour, and fashion will come with an ethical price tag. Arslan eventually won his right to a half-hour break and a five-day work week, but he was also laid off shortly after.

16
The Architecture of Aversion

Unlike many parts of the world where social housing is synonymous with systemic neglect and poverty, most Singaporeans view public housing as a normal standard of living. These homes are high-rise apartment buildings managed by the Housing and Development Board and are thus often referred to as HDB flats. Situated in self-contained towns with public amenities such as schools, a well-connected public transport network, and shops, HDB housing contrasts sharply with Western models, which are often concentrated in lower-income areas. The residents living in HDB flats are a mixed-income community. In this regard, HDB flats are not perceived as welfare housing, but as the fundamental architecture of a well-planned nation.

I only realised how unique Singaporeans' perception of social housing was during a casual conversation with a colleague from Edinburgh. She had just visited Singapore and remarked, with visible discomfort, how she was affected by the sight of many social housing buildings. As our conversation continued, it became clear to me that much of her discomfort stemmed from the Western perception of social housing, largely shaped by the United Kingdom's public housing. Recalling some of the council housing I have seen in Edinburgh and the United Kingdom, I began to understand her less-than-positive perception of social housing. In most high-income economy countries, with a few exceptions such as Austria, Denmark, and the Netherlands, social housing carries a reputation for social dysfunction and poverty.

In Singapore, social housing is something altogether different: over 80% of the population lives in HDB flats. These units span across income levels and are governed by a model that blends ownership with public provision. The class distribution of residents living in HDB flats is relatively flat. My colleague's comments drew my attention to a deeper bias that pervades the universal impression of social housing. That conversation prompted my curiosity: how could some of the world's most developed, resource-rich, and technologically advanced countries still be trapped by this limiting perception of social housing, in which it is often an afterthought for inhabitants with the fewest resources?

The answer lies in the fact that, in many countries, the stigma surrounding social housing resulted from architectural and political oversights. The transition from 'working-class housing' to segregated 'poverty traps' was steered by historical and systemic factors. In the United States, the segregation in public housing was a consequence of an intentional, racially coded policy. Baltimore passed the country's first racial-zoning ordinance, making it illegal for African Americans to live in predominantly white neighbourhoods. It was a racist response to George McMechen's, an African American graduate of Yale Law School, move into an affluent, all-white neighbourhood in Baltimore, Maryland. Other cities throughout the country followed suit, adopting similar laws, and thus, racial zoning was normalised.

Redlining in the United States systematically denied mortgages and investment in Black neighbourhoods, forcing residents into limited housing options, often public housing. In addition, public housing was often built in already declining, racially segregated neighbourhoods. Redlining was instrumental in obstructing pathways to wealth accumulation, thereby further impoverishing the families who lived there. When jobs began to vanish due to deindustrialisation in the 1970s, many residents of public housing, cut off from upward mobility and only surrounded by failing infrastructure, became what sociologist William Julius Wilson called 'the truly disadvantaged'. Racial bias was the primary cause of racial inequality in housing, health, and economic opportunities that affected generations.

In the UK, the problems with social housing stemmed from an ideological misstep that shifted the view of social housing from a public provision for the working population to a 'tenure of last resort'. During the Thatcher administration, a well-intentioned but ultimately short-sighted policy, the 'Right to Buy' scheme, was introduced. Tenants in council housing could buy their homes at generous discounts, an offer many took up. But the units of council housing sold were never adequately replaced, resulting in a severe depletion in available social housing. Former council homes sold under the scheme were often also rented back to tenants at higher prices. The remaining council housing became concentrated in less desirable areas, with most of it consisting of poorly maintained flats. With the decline of traditional industries in northern towns and former mining communities, those council housing areas became isolated spaces for families who were less socially and economically mobile. Council housing, which was once an emblem of a steadfast welfare system aimed at providing high-quality, long-term, and affordable housing for, as quoted in the 1946 New Towns Act, 'working man, the doctor and the clergyman', became an afterthought housing option for lower-income households. The policy failure led to lasting stigma and underinvestment in council homes.

In France, the alienation of communities living in social housing also resulted from flawed urban planning doctrines. Modern housing planning in France was notably influenced by, though rarely aligned with, Le Corbusier's vision of the 'Radiant City'. Social housing developments were built with strict adherence to functional principles, separating residential, industrial, and commercial functions into distinct zones. The approach was conceptualised as a solution to overcrowding and pollution in industrialised France. In social housing zones, street-level activities were obliterated to avoid congestion and improve efficiency. But it also created a sterile, disorienting environment that lacked community interaction. With limited employment opportunities in residential zones and low transport connectivity, residents were often socially, economically, and hence symbolically cut off. These planning decisions, which prioritised rapid, cost-effective, and standardised construction, were, for many critics, a major cause of the social fragmentation and alienation that came to define the modern French *banlieue*. Residents of the *banlieue* are often regarded as 'others': visible only during riots or moments of unrest, rarely seen as integral parts of the urban city.

New studies in the late 20th and early 21st centuries have shown that isolationist approaches, characterised by large, concentrated, and segregated developments, compound inequality rather than alleviate it. When housing estates are designed with little regard for social interaction, crime often arises. Open spaces within social housing estates tend to be afterthoughts: undefined voids between buildings rather than spaces for communal activities. Social housing zones are also located far from job centres, causing significant, compounded barriers to employment, education, and childcare. A lack of reliable, affordable transportation and access to grocery stores and fresh produce often intensifies residents' challenges, especially for mothers, older adults, and people with limited mobility.

Social housing estates face a systemic cycle of disinvestment, neglect, and stigma. In part, it is because policymakers often assume social housing is temporary. That viewpoint prevents long-term investment and leads to underfunding and neglect. These assumptions reinforce its stigma. The tragic Grenfell Tower fire in London is a harrowing reminder of the devastating consequences of negative or erroneous perceptions of social housing.

But, Vienna, on the other hand, offers a compelling model of what tenure-blind, publicly committed housing can achieve. Since the 1920s, Vienna's housing philosophy has rested on a universalist idea: that access to good housing is a social right. Its municipal housing serves a wide range of residents, not just those in need but also middle-income residents. As policies focus on long-term affordability and integration rather than forcing residents to move to private housing, contracts remain valid as residents' incomes rise. In this way, the social housing estate maintains a rich socioeconomic mix. Vienna's social housing estates are well integrated with transport networks, green spaces, schools, and public services. There are recent pressures due to housing shortages, market changes, and the influx of migrants. However, Vienna's social housing model is a positive example of what can happen when it is treated as national infrastructure rather than welfare provision.

A social housing estate that I enjoyed visiting whenever I am in London was the Brunswick Centre. Nestled in Bloomsbury, Central London, the residential complex was conceived as a mixed-use social housing estate, with around 400 social housing apartments managed by Camden Council. There is a continuous flow of activity throughout the day, giving the estate a vibrancy and a sense of safety that many monofunctional housing estates lack. The presence of 'eyes on the street', as American-Canadian theorist and journalist Jane Jacobs might say, discourages the isolation and neglect that often befall segregated social housing zones.

But the Brunswick Centre was originally envisioned as a private luxury development, marking an early experiment in blending retail and residential uses. The flats were built to high standards, many with balconies, and served by a combined heat and power system. But when the project failed to attract enough private buyers, and its developer eventually went bankrupt, Camden Council stepped in. The Council leased the residential portion on a 99-year contract, turning it into social housing for existing tenants. In a twist of irony, the developer's bankruptcy enabled Camden Council to adopt a tenure-blind social housing model. More importantly, Camden Council learned from Thatcher's past mistakes and developed guidelines that capped the number of units eligible for private ownership under the 'Right to Buy' scheme. Today, only about 25% of the units have been sold, with the remaining occupied by long-term tenants.

On a visit to Brunswick Centre in 2024, I discovered that it is not immune to gentrification; larger chain stores and eateries have replaced some of the local shops I used to frequent. Despite that, it was still heartening to see residents, families, and older adults interacting in the central square. The tenure-blind social housing approach appears to have helped the estate maintain a balanced social mix. Both Vienna and the Camden Council resist the notion that social housing is merely transitional and implement policies with a long-term view. While a tenure-blind social housing model may seem costly, the dividends, such as socially cohesive neighbourhoods, vibrant street activities, and dignified living conditions, that a city may reap are immeasurable.

An Afternote

Although Singapore's public housing model is often held up as a rare success in avoiding the stigma seen in Western systems, it is not without emerging strains. Rising resale prices and longer waiting times have begun to test the government's original promise of affordability. Its 99-year lease model also introduces a growing tension as these housing estates age. As the value of these estates declines, the long-held belief that such homes function as shelter and wealth-building is also eroding. In recent decades, many HDB flat leaseholders have increasingly treated their units as income-generating assets through rental. This shift has led to more units occupied by transient tenants rather than long-term residents. Such a shift is also subtly altering the social composition of HDB estates, once designed to foster stable, community-rooted living.

Decoding Our Biases

The stories in the preceding chapters are like planets orbiting the sun. Although the subject matters vary, they are all held together by a reality: cognitive biases are an inherent and hence unavoidable aspect of our cognition. Because we all perceive through subconscious filters, one practical way to mitigate their impact is to acknowledge that our actions, decisions, and judgments are suboptimal. To foster that awareness, we first need to acquaint ourselves with how multifarious biases influence our judgments and decision-making in varied situations. In the following section, I grouped biases into four commonly encountered situations: making decisions, interacting with others, facing moral and ethical dilemmas, and experiencing intense emotions.

17
Decision-Making Biases

Cognitive shortcuts, also known as heuristics, are automatic mental processes that help us navigate complex information by drawing on past experiences and social cues. These shortcuts allow us to make decisions efficiently and are often an instinctive way to make sense of our surroundings. In short, mental shortcuts are essential components of human reasoning that allow us to process information and make decisions. However, when a situation demands slower, more deliberate reasoning, our reliance on these shortcuts often leads to biased outcomes, and we are rarely aware that we are holding distorted perceptions. Our oblivion to the downside of heuristics becomes a liability as society grows more complex amid rapid technological change, global connectivity, and a ceaseless flow of information. These shortcuts are often insufficient for navigating volatile, uncertain, complex, and ambiguous conditions, often referred to as a VUCA world. This is simply because our cognitive processes rely on past patterns, limited information, and implicit assumptions that often do not hold in rapidly changing contexts.

Despite that, we are relying even more heavily on cognitive shortcuts when confronting VUCA conditions. This is in part driven by the demands of the knowledge economy. Technological, social, and economic systems have become increasingly interconnected, requiring individuals with an extensive 'vertical' expertise to manage them. As a result, the modern economy rewards individuals with deep over broad specialisation. A workforce of specialists has become a key advantage for nations and businesses trying to stay ahead; we are increasingly hired and valued for a narrow expertise. The demand for vertical mastery also gave rise to siloed work designs. In such environments, employees are rarely encouraged to explore beyond their immediate assigned role and expertise. A company's hyper-focus on specialisation, combined with relentless pressure for speed, implicitly motivates employees to rely on mental shortcuts. Over time, this environment fosters biased thinking.

The following biases are among the most common cognitive traps in decision-making, often distorting our reasoning without our realising it.

Confirmation Bias

Confirmation bias is our tendency to seek out and give greater weight to information that supports our existing beliefs, while ignoring or dismissing information and reasoning that contradict them. The flat-earthers who set out on a sea voyage to find the edge of the world chose to use the compass as their navigation tool, whose very function relies on a spherical Earth. Such a dissonant choice reveals confirmation bias in their decision-making. They gave greater weight to their chosen belief than to the logical conflict of using a compass. Confirmation bias may also have contributed to the high incidence of scams in Singapore. Victims, due to ingrained trust in authority, might have placed considerable importance on messages that appeared to be from government institutions or banks. Led by confirmation bias, these individuals reinforced their belief in the messages' legitimacy, causing them to overlook obvious red flags. Similarly, the 2008 mortgage crisis could be linked to confirmation bias among investors and regulators who believed that housing prices would always increase and that mortgage-backed securities were therefore safe. As a result, investors, lenders, and even policymakers dismissed growing evidence of risky mortgages and mounting defaults.

Overconfidence Bias

The overconfidence effect is a cognitive bias in which a person's subjective confidence in their judgments reliably exceeds the objective accuracy of those judgments. This bias has been consistently demonstrated in numerous research studies in which participants are asked to report their certainty in specific judgments or answers across different domains. Respondents often overestimate their driving skills, general knowledge, and sports abilities.

Overconfidence bias, particularly in the form of planning fallacy, is a primary contributor to our poor estimates of how long tasks will take. It also manifests in our illusion of control, where we may feel we have more influence over outcomes than we actually do. It may be an underlying cause of why individuals fall deeper into 'pig-butchering' scam tactics, with victims remaining in disbelief that they have been tricked. Their disbelief reflects a common dismissal: 'it won't happen to me.' In Singapore's case, the country's low crime rate and orderliness could have bolstered victims' overconfidence, leading them to believe that scams were less likely to occur in Singapore than in other countries. Due to overconfidence bias, we frequently attribute positive results solely to our skills and capacity. Investors who believe their investment returns stem from their insight and skills may subsequently overlook the inherent risks of stocks. The 1987 Black Monday Crash notably exemplified how overconfident investors placed excessive faith in automated risk-management systems and left no provisions for risks and errors.

Sunk Cost Fallacy

Individuals often succumb to this psychological phenomenon in which they are reluctant to abandon a course of action or a flawed strategy because they are emotionally attached to the weight of their prior investments and efforts. When we persist in a course of action that is evidently futile, we have likely succumbed to the sunk cost fallacy. The audit findings that SPH Media inflated its circulation numbers suggest a questionable decision shackled to an outmoded business model. The misreporting hints at a classic sunk-cost trap. Rather than embracing the realities of digital media and adopting new strategies to mitigate the natural decline of print readership and advertising revenue, the proponents chose to prop up the declining business model.

Anchoring Bias

Anchoring bias is a cognitive phenomenon in which our judgments or decisions are influenced by an initial observation, piece of information, or experience (the anchor). Anchoring bias is clearly evident in the case of 'Chinese Restaurant Syndrome'. MSG's association with Chinese restaurants, at a time of heightened cultural suspicion, became a critical hook for public anxieties. Once that negative health association was anchored to Chinese restaurants, the subsequent scientific rebuttals against the myth of MSG struggled to gain traction.

Anchoring bias is especially visible in urban policymaking, where fiscal value often becomes the dominant reference point for many planning decisions. As noted by Binyamin Appelbaum, cities in the U.S. often fall over themselves to subsidise sports arenas and other high-profile projects because these initiatives are framed as economically productive and revenue-generating. That fiscal lens becomes the anchor: alternative considerations, such as minimising inequality, improving social cohesion, or enhancing affordability, all of which are essential to a vibrant, inclusive, and truly sustainable urban life, are routinely judged against it and dismissed as too costly or too complex. Anchoring urban planning in fiscal value persists in many governments worldwide. Focusing on social health in urban planning is often dismissed, even when its long-term benefits may far outweigh any immediate economic returns.

The historical account of *The Affair of the Diamond Necklace* is also a compelling lesson on how anchoring bias influences judgments in trials. When Madame de La Motte and her accomplices stole a necklace originally commissioned for Marie Antoinette, the public immediately believed Marie Antoinette was the true instigator of the theft. Even after Marie Antoinette was proven innocent at trial, public perception remained unchanged. Their perception of her guilt was anchored in Marie Antoinette's reputation for lavish spending. Unsurprisingly, modern-day spin doctors for politicians are well aware of how to leverage anchoring bias to ruin opponents' reputations or sway public opinion.

In salary negotiations, the starting salary offer can have a strong anchoring effect on a young graduate's economic mobility. Subsequent salaries are often set based on previous salaries rather than on a candidate's competence or scope of work.

Availability Heuristic

The availability heuristic leads us to rely on the most immediate information, observations, or knowledge readily available in our memory when making decisions. It is a phenomenon that explains the increase in our fear of flying after a plane crash. Food product marketers understand how the availability heuristic influences consumers' perceptions and often leverage it in their product label designs. Thus, processed foods often carry labels with words like 'Innocent', 'Pure', and 'Natural', all of which suggest healthy options.

When the Gaza War broke out, social media platforms like TikTok and Instagram became conduits for a relentless stream of visceral depictions of the suffering of victims from both sides. That streamed content might have potently influenced viewers' judgments about the conflict's ethical significance. A graphic, emotionally charged video, regardless of its accuracy, stays far more 'available' in our memory than a detailed analysis, and can shape our opinions almost instantly. Availability heuristics trick our brain into mistaking the most vivid information as the representative truth of the conflict.

The availability heuristic, through vivid, convincing, and extreme narratives, can accelerate radicalisation, pushing individuals to abandon logical reasoning. It is plausible that, in Michael Gloss's case, an echo chamber of emotionally evocative messages and videos might have led him to transform from an anti-war advocate into a mercenary fighter against Ukraine.

Optimism Bias

Optimism bias refers to our tendency to overestimate the likelihood of positive events happening to us and to underestimate the likelihood of negative events happening. In simpler terms, optimism bias causes us to underestimate personal risk and overestimate positive future outcomes, even when the evidence before us suggests otherwise. In the case of SPH Media, optimism bias could have been a significant psychological factor that enabled the culpable protagonists to continue inflating print circulation numbers. Singapore's low crime rate might have bolstered scam victims' optimism, leading them to believe that they are less likely to be cheated. Optimism bias often manifests as an unquestioning sense of positivity. It is common in business and personal decision-making, where we often assume that failure, illness, or economic downturns will strike elsewhere. The truth is, we are less cautious in nature, not because we are reckless, but because we are convinced that we are less exposed to negative encounters.

18
Social Perception Biases

Social perception biases are the cognitive shortcuts we use to interpret and make sense of the behaviours of those around us. These perceptions are forged through socialisation, an influential process by which we acquire our identity, personality, and conscience. In a community, we learn to cooperate and respect a social order that ensures continuity. Socialisation is vital to order and collective growth, as it ensures that norms and values are transmitted across generations. But it is also the primary vehicle for imparting perception biases.

To understand this relationship, we must recognise that much of how we see the world is through our cultural lens. We develop this perceptive lens through socialisation, and that lens defines what is considered normal or acceptable. This process involves gradually learning and internalising the unwritten rules that define acceptable behaviours within a group. Those unwritten rules are heavily influenced by familial upbringing, cultural and religious beliefs, and socioeconomic conditions. Subconsciously, our internalised perceptions become our yardstick for interpreting and judging others' actions and motivations. This is where social perception bias occurs: while these shortcuts allow us to navigate our own community with ease, they often fail when applied to environments outside of it. Instead, our social perceptions may produce inaccurate impressions that lead to erroneous, and occasionally harmful, conclusions.

In-group Bias

In-group bias, the tendency to favour one's own group over others, is often attributed to the work of sociologist William Graham Sumner. He posited that humans are a species that naturally form groups and tend to favour their own group over others. In-group bias is thought to have roots in our evolutionary past, in which human survival depended heavily on group cohesion to secure scarce resources and defend against threats. Favouring one's own members over outsiders maximises the chances of survival for one's own kind. This evolutionary instinct for survival may have persisted into modern times, manifesting as various in-group biases. Like most social perception biases, in-group bias is a double-edged sword. While 'sticking together' deepens community bonds and fosters a collaborative spirit, we may often do so at the expense of principles of fairness and inclusivity, exacerbating intergroup conflict.

One of the most heated discourses of our times that is attributable to in-group bias is the argument for and against the representation and belonging of LGBTQ+ athletes in sports. Martina Navratilova's call for a separate 'open' or 'trans' category so that all, including transgender athletes, can participate in sports competitions. But her argument for preserving the integrity of the female category for solely cis-women athletes is panned by some LGBTQ+ advocacy groups as discriminatory. Indeed, it is a complex issue that requires civil, objective dialogue. But in-group bias can prevent both sides from reaching a fair and inclusive solution. When we favour only our own advocacy, dig in on our cause, and dismiss or disparage outsiders, we are less likely to arrive at any nuanced, bilateral solutions.

The Israel-Palestine conflict is not merely a geopolitical tussle over territorial rights and border security, but one that is also intertwined with religious and cultural narratives. Strong in-group loyalties on both sides promulgate their moral arguments surrounding the conflict, deepen opposing views and reinforce further divisions. When protestors called for greater reflection on Israel's humanitarian violations, they were immediately shut down as pro-Hamas or antisemitic.

A more common example of in-group bias occurs in our workplace. Hiring managers often, unconsciously, favour candidates who mirror their own identity, whether through shared cultural or educational backgrounds, similar religious or political beliefs, or even personal commonalities that create an immediate connection. Naturally, in-group bias limits diversity in hiring and sometimes misses out on well-qualified talent simply because those candidates fall outside the hirer's perceived 'in-group'.

Groupthink

Groupthink happens when members in a group or community, motivated by in-group loyalty and the desire to fit in, self-censor and suppress dissenting views. This tendency to preserve a group's ideals and unity often leads to poor decision-making, as it fails to consider alternative arguments. This flawed psychological process was first described by Irving Janis, based on his observations and analysis of major U.S. foreign policy fiascoes.

Groupthink could be one reason SPH Media misreported its print circulation numbers. Given that the malpractice persisted for nearly 18 months, it suggests that employees, whether voluntarily or otherwise, helped conceal it. It is plausible that many employees were under immense pressure to maintain a cohesive front (perhaps out of fear of losing their jobs?) and thus collectively ignored the unethical and counter-strategic nature of the practice.

The Space Shuttle Challenger disaster is a well-known and sobering reminder of the dangers of groupthink. The engineers' warnings about faulty O-rings were not properly communicated or acted upon to meet the high-stakes launch deadlines. In high-stakes situations, unity is a critical linchpin of group survival. Yet counterintuitively, the pressure to project a unified front often impels individuals to conform rigidly.

Although conflict and crisis are powerful catalysts for unifying people, they may also, counterproductively, exacerbate flawed thinking. In a crisis, the urgent need for a unified front may override critical analysis, a key factor in effectively mitigating challenges. Immediately after the September 11, 2001, terrorist attacks, a climate of intense patriotism and national unity led to the criticism and marginalisation of anyone who questioned or scrutinised the U.S. government's reactions to the attacks. Americans who dissented against the U.S. invasion of Iraq in 2003 were labelled as unpatriotic.

Ethnocentric Bias

Ethnocentrism is closely related to in-group bias. The term ethnocentrism was first coined by Ludwig Gumplowicz, who used it in at least eight publications before William Graham Sumner popularised the concept in his widely read book, Folkways, in 1906. Gumplowicz viewed ethnocentrism as a phenomenon akin to geocentrism (the belief that the Earth is at the centre of the universe) and anthropocentrism (the belief that humans are at the centre of the universe), but focused on one's own ethnic group, nation, or people. He noted many historical examples of this bias: Aristotle's claim of Greek superiority over 'deficient' outsiders, Hegel's assertion of German godlike status, the French conviction of their unique civilising mission, the Chinese perception of their nation as the world's epicentre, and the Jewish belief in their status as a chosen people. In addition, Gumplowicz also noted that many ethnic groups hold ethnocentric religious myths, often assuming the first human couple originated in their own ethnic group.

Gastronationalism, which emphasises the superiority of one nation's cuisine, can be considered a mild manifestation of ethnocentric ideology. Ethnocentrism may have contributed to the persistence of the long-running MSG hoax, fueled by suspicion or dismissal of foreign culinary dishes. It is also evident in Italy's outrage over Professor Alberto Grandi's research claims that some of Italy's prided dishes, such as Carbonara and pizza, were not originally Italian.

Likewise, the indignation expressed by Malaysian netizens when Singapore's hawker food was inscribed on UNESCO's Representative List of the Intangible Cultural Heritage of Humanity was likely an ethnocentric response. Malaysians are partly right to claim their hawker fare as authentic. While many dishes share the same names across both countries, they have also evolved into distinct culinary identities. The diverse preparation methods and flavour profiles of hawker dishes in Malaysia and Singapore today result from diasporic immigrant communities adapting their recipes to local tastes. But ethnocentrism led netizens to fight over claims to authenticity, overshadowing the shared human history of migration.

Colonial discrimination was rooted in ethnocentrism, using perceived technological and moral advantages as a pretext for subjugation. In our modern times, ethnocentrism continues to influence the motivations of war and violent conflicts heavily. As observed in the Israel-Gaza conflict, ethnocentric religious narratives were frequently cited and disseminated across social media platforms as justification for their war actions.

Stereotyping

Stereotype bias occurs when we use categorical generalisations to evaluate individuals, attributing specific traits or behaviours to them only because they belong to a particular social group. The LGBTQ+ community, for example, is often a subject of stereotype bias. In fact, discrimination against the LGBTQ+ community often is rooted in stereotypes and in-group biases. Many people lack personal, firsthand interactions with openly LGBTQ+ individuals and often rely on the concept of heteronormativity as the default state of all other humans. Individuals who do not meet this expectation are often stereotyped based on limiting representations from the media, politics, and religion.

In this regard, the motivations of LGBTQ+ activism are often obscured by the stereotyped generalisations of LGBTQ+ people. Very often, the reductive stereotyped notion that LGBTQ+ people are inherently transgressive or promiscuous gives credence to false accusations that LGBTQ+ activism threatens to erode religious values and social order.

Another example of stereotyping is the widespread and outdated assumption that women are less suited for STEM careers. Such a stereotyped view has historically influenced hiring biases and workplace dynamics.

Fundamental Attribution Error

Besides judging others by their association with a community or group, we also judge others by their disposition without considering their situation. What that means is we tend to attribute what we observe in others to their personality traits, character, or attitudes. The fundamental attribution error refers to our tendency to judge ourselves situationally, especially when our actions fall short of expectations (or when we fail), and to judge others dispositionally when their expected behaviours fall short.

To make it easier to understand, let me share my initial experiences as a pedestrian at zebra crossings when I first moved to Italy. I noticed drivers there tend to slow down much closer to the crossings than I am used to in other countries. Sometimes, they would not even stop. In those moments, I would instinctively consider those drivers rude or selfish, even though I did not know them personally and thus was not privy to their situation as they approached the crossing. In those instances, I was making a fundamental attribution error by assuming their behaviour, of failing to slow down at the crossing, results from their character.

This bias is best illustrated by a classic study in which participants tried to teach math to a student (who was actually a member of the research team posing as a student). The researcher then informed the participant that their student had either performed well or poorly on a math test. When a student did well, the teaching participant attributed the other student's success to their own great instructional skills. However, when a student performed poorly, the teaching participant attributed the failure solely to that student. In this classic study, the behaviour was termed self-serving attribution.

The fundamental attribution error may engender apathy towards inequality: we tend to emphasise the character shortcomings of people facing poverty rather than examine systemic barriers that might have caused the imbalance. For the same reason, we are less likely to consider unemployment, homelessness, and even drug addiction as consequences of systemic, social dysfunctions. This bias is strikingly evident in arguments against social assistance, which often contend that extensive social benefits create a culture of dependency. In this regard, the fundamental attribution error's influence on the erroneous perceptions of social inequality offers another explanation why policymakers continue to anchor big-ticket commercial projects in urban development, resulting in the allocation of more land to commercial and private housing than to social housing.

This bias is most evident in British social policies on property ownership during Prime Minister Margaret Thatcher's rule. In that period, the prevailing perception was that everyone would strive to move from social housing to private property. That error in judgment effectively transformed council housing in Britain into a perceived symbol of personal failure, leading to its steady decline and the eventual marginalisation of families who were unable to afford private housing and thus forced to remain on council estates.

Halo Effect

While the fundamental attribution error describes our tendency to overemphasise internal traits, such as personality and temperament, when judging others' negative behaviours, the halo effect is a different cognitive bias in which our positive impression of an individual, organisation, or brand influences our perception of their unrelated characteristics.

The classic saying 'first impressions count' perfectly explains why first impressions are critical, as they can trigger the halo effect. During job interviews, an initial positive impression of a candidate may strongly influence the hirer's decision. The halo effect often leads voters to form a positive impression of successful business leaders running for office; voters erroneously conflate successful entrepreneurship with leadership acumen. Elon Musk is often cited as a visionary for his rapid rise in wealth through his business ventures. Despite his overt, erratic emotional outbursts, his supporters continue to admire him and justify his unrestrained antisocial behaviour as a positive trait of a leader unafraid to express his thoughts.

Companies often leverage the halo effect to shape consumer perception. By associating themselves with positive social causes, using specific, emotionally resonant imagery, or employing strategic colour palettes, companies can create a positive aura. The continued desirability of luxury goods, even amid repeated scandals over ethical labour breaches, is a fine example of how luxury houses leverage the halo effect, projecting an image of quality, ethics, and trust through sophisticated marketing.

The halo effect can also help individuals get off scot-free and face less scrutiny for their negative actions. When positive perceptions reduce moral scrutiny, those benefiting from the halo effect may feel implicitly entitled to engage in questionable or unethical behaviour. The halo effect can thus evoke moral licensing: people excuse misconduct because they admire the person. A well-known illustration of the halo effect's incidental role in moral licensing comes from Donald Trump's now-infamous remark during the 2016 campaign, when he claimed he 'could stand in the middle of Fifth Avenue and shoot somebody' without losing any voters. The remark illustrates how the halo effect can blur moral boundaries. When glowing approval becomes unconditional, it risks being internalised as tacit permission, thereby paving the way for moral licensing.

Bandwagon Effect

The bandwagon effect is a cognitive bias in which people adopt behaviours, beliefs, or preferences because many others are doing the same. The effect is often driven by our desire to fit in or be on the 'winning' side. In part, it stems from anxiety over or a desire for validation within social groups. Often, these feelings, commonly observed and defined in modern social media parlance as the fear of missing out (FOMO), lead us to override logic, such as ignoring individual judgment or contrary information. Social media platforms' algorithms are specifically designed to leverage this cognitive bias, accelerating the spread of content that shows potential traction by creating popularity feedback loops. As a result, these platforms serve as highly efficient tools for marketers and politicians in devising campaigns that help them gain more followers or project a sense of majority or popular support.

The heated reaction to Michael Petraeus's critique of former President Halimah Yacob illustrates how the bandwagon effect can steer public debate. Through his blog, *The Critical Spectator*, Petraeus cultivated a following by presenting himself as a blunt, no-nonsense commentator who valued pragmatism over ideology. His persona resonated with Singapore's self-image as a secular, rational society; agreeing with him feels like a mark of critical thinking. By framing Yacob's humanitarian concern for Gaza as religiously driven and centring his critique on Hamas, Petraeus drew readers into a 'pick a side' situation. The growing appearance of consensus lent his views credibility, prompting more supporters to echo his argument and crowd out Yacob's original humanitarian message.

Spotlight Effect

The spotlight effect is the tendency to believe that our actions, appearance, or errors are under constant, intense scrutiny by others. This bias is often linked to egocentric bias, in which our natural tendency to view the world from our own perspective also leads us to overemphasise our own actions and appearance, falsely believing others notice us more than they do. It is a widely observed social phenomenon among teenagers, characterised by a heightened self-consciousness about their clothing, speech, and actions. As a result, the spotlight effect affects our self-identity in many ways. Our political and social stances, as well as our consumption choices, which may be motivated by a sense of being under constant scrutiny, often lead us to behave in ways we believe others expect of us. It is a bias that manifests as a consciousness to present a particular image of ourselves to the world. While the spotlight effect is often harmless, it has become our Achilles' heel in the age of misinformation warfare. Agents seeking to spread divisiveness and misinformation can exploit our inherent need for social approval by prompting us to 'like' or 'repost' their content, thereby amplifying their misinformation and trapping us in their echo chambers.

19
Moral Biases

Relying on mental shortcuts is often efficient and reasonably accurate in handling complex information, and this rule-of-thumb thinking does not always distort our judgments. But as we have discovered, it can foster systematic errors that lead to suboptimal actions and, in some cases, moral lapses. These shortcuts harden into biases and unconscious attitudes that shape our thoughts, decisions, and actions. Such unconscious, deeply ingrained preferences are what psychologists call implicit biases: automatic reactions, responses, and associations that operate beneath our conscious awareness. As these biases influence how we judge right and wrong and what we interpret as fair and responsible, they take on a moral dimension and sometimes even conflict with our own ethical standards. For this reason, I group them under moral biases.

Status Quo Bias

A status quo bias, or default bias, is a cognitive bias that leads people to prefer maintaining the status quo. Any change from that existing state is often perceived as negative or undesirable. This bias differs from our rational preference for the status quo when it is more beneficial than the available alternatives, or when we lack sufficient information to make a reasonably sound judgment about changing. Status quo bias is frequently encountered in the workplace, where business leaders are averse to challenging established or legacy practices within their organisations. Inflating print circulation figures was clearly neither a valid nor a strategic consideration for SPH Media's long-term growth. Yet the decision to anchor to SPH Media's legacy business model, extracting advertising revenue from the declining print media business, may have stemmed from status quo bias. Similarly, status quo bias is evident in Kodak's resistance to digital photography, despite having ironically invented one of the first digital cameras. Likewise, BlackBerry's dismissal of touchscreen technology as a novelty was a misstep of status quo bias. In all of these cases, leadership chose comfort derived from running the 'business as usual'.

Status quo bias is also evident in politics; political parties often continue to cling to narratives and ideologies that are increasingly out of touch with reality. Immigration is a clear example. Research has found that left-leaning parties often speak in favour of open immigration, even though they usually govern within tight economic, demographic, and legal constraints that leave little room for favourable change for immigrants. This contrast between intention and action is also known as the liberal paradox, where the ethos of liberal parties fails to alter the status quo of strict immigration controls. Yet many liberal politicians continue to defend immigration in moral and absolutist terms, even as their actual policies increasingly resemble those of their conservative opponents. The political reluctance on the left to acknowledge this reality reflects a subtler form of status quo bias: preserving a moral self-image even as policies are much more aligned with constraining immigration. Status quo bias often locks political parties into narratives that no longer match lived realities.

During the Gaza-Israel conflict, the Israeli right-wing relied on a long-standing strategy of framing criticism of its military actions as antisemitic. The persistence of this deflection is reinforced by a collective sense of victimhood, rooted in a long history of Jewish persecution, that has become central to Israel's national identity. Unfortunately, status quo bias confines Israeli right-wing leaders to continue with this narrative, in defence of their aggressive and flagrant occupation policies in Gaza. Such an approach risks weakening Israel's credibility and international legitimacy and may even make it harder to defend itself when genuine antisemitism arises.

Appelbaum's critique of U.S. municipal governments in his *New York Times* op-ed illustrates status quo bias in action. Cities continue to prioritise stadiums as 'fiscal anchors' only because it is a model that has been accepted and repeatedly deployed. The bias fostered a habitual reliance on high-profile projects for urban development. This approach often crowds out alternative, human-centric considerations, like affordable housing or public spaces, that could yield more sustainable social and economic benefits. In this way, the status quo traps policymakers into repeating familiar patterns, even when those patterns no longer serve the public effectively.

Introspection Illusion Bias

The introspection illusion bias describes how we readily recognise biased thinking and actions from others while remaining oblivious to the same biases in ourselves. This cognitive bias was defined by social psychologist Emily Pronin and her colleagues. The irony is that we are unaware of it. It also means that as I point out the effects of bias in this book, I, too, am writing from a biased viewpoint! The introspection illusion bias was clearly a contributing factor to the high incidence of scams in Singapore and, indeed, in scam situations elsewhere in the world. Despite widespread reports of scams, we can all easily fall prey to them because we tend to view our own perceptions and judgments as rational, accurate, and unbiased. Similarly, the Flat Earthers who set out to find the edge of the world viewed their own perspective as objective reality, leading to the expedition's fiasco. Their persistent attempts to evade the authorities so they could continue their search were evidently influenced by the introspection illusion bias. Extremists, when radicalising recruits to their ideologies, often exploit their victims' limited perspectives and a lack of introspection by luring them into an insular echo chamber that offers little room for critical self-reflection.

Petraeus' argument against former President Yacob was riddled with fallacies, such as whataboutism and narratives of collective guilt, and was shaped by selective framing, unchecked assumptions, and flawed ideologies. That he did not even question his own flawed reasoning as a self-styled 'critical spectator' is a clear example of the introspection illusion bias. The inconsistency between his carefully cultivated persona of objectivity and the partiality of his arguments becomes less puzzling in the context of this bias.

Moral Licensing

Moral licensing is a psychological trade-off in which we allow ourselves to act unethically or immorally because of past good deeds. Each of us subconsciously keeps a mental account of our good deeds, which influences our subsequent ethical and moral decisions. We are more likely to allow or justify our subsequent bad deeds when we feel we have built up moral credit. The idea of tokenism is a derivative of moral licensing. The widely used terms like pinkwashing and greenwashing are forms of tokenism, often directed at companies that respectively adopt them as LGBTQ+ and environmentally friendly marketing tactics to bolster a positive social image.

The recent controversies surrounding B Corp certification are rife with accusations of moral licensing. The certification body has faced accusations of greenwashing for certifying companies such as Nestlé's Nespresso, which is alleged to have a poor human rights record. Nestlé's certification as a B Corp sparked backlash and led companies, including Dr Bronner's, to withdraw from the program. In another major complaint, employees accused BrewDog, also a B Corp-certified company, of instilling a culture of fear in the organisation. BrewDog eventually lost its certification.

Amazon often launches highly polished feel-good advertising campaigns that focus on emotional storytelling about kindness and human connections. It also runs campaigns that emphasise its commitment to community, sustainability, disaster relief, education, and social inclusion. At first glance, Amazon's focus on 'feel-good' storytelling seems paradoxical amid persistent accusations of its exploitative labour practices; one might wonder why the company would risk making these messages ring hollow or provoke backlash when they are clearly dissonant with the allegations. From a moral-licensing perspective, these 'feel-good' storytelling campaigns may serve a strategic psychological purpose. Perhaps Amazon understands that for the broader public, a bold, curated message highlighting 'good deeds' can function as a moral offset. By reminding and convincing the audience that the company has done something 'good enough', these advertisements offer consumers a cognitive shield that helps them maintain their patronage despite Amazon's alleged workplace toxicity.

In the colonial period, European powers' self-perception of moral superiority and their good intentions to bring civilisation, Christianity, and progress to the colonies served as a moral justification for their exploitative measures. Moral trade-offs also play out every day in grocery aisles: shoppers, as research on consumer decision-making and psychology notes, justify indulging in junk food or unsustainable purchases as a form of self-reward for their environmentally friendly act of using a tote bag.

Just-World Hypothesis

Another cognitive bias that influences our ethical and moral judgments is our belief that the world is fair and that all good deeds are rewarded while bad deeds are punished. With this perspective, we tend to believe that misfortune befalls individuals because they deserve it. The just-world hypothesis often manifests as victim-blaming. In reality, it is a defence mechanism that helps us reduce anxiety and maintain the feeling that the world is predictable. But it also causes us to overlook external factors, such as structural injustices, when assessing an individual's unfortunate circumstances. This way of thinking fosters apathy toward social issues such as income inequality and discrimination, shifting our attention away from broader social forces. In that same manner, the just-world hypothesis reinforces our faith in a meritocratic system that appears fair, even when it is not. Similarly, it distorts our view of the welfare state; we hold the misconception that social support fosters dependence rather than helping address the unequal starting conditions of the underserved.

The just world hypothesis is not confined to abstract moral reasoning; it surfaces repeatedly in how societies respond to suffering. In the context of the Israel-Gaza conflict, some political arguments place moral responsibility for the deaths of Palestinian civilians on Palestinian's choice of leadership. Policymakers have often viewed HIV/AIDS as a disease that victims brought upon themselves. Often, the lack of political will to allocate land for social housing stems from the belief that those in need are responsible for their own precarious situations. In all three cases, the influence of the just-world hypothesis is unmistakable, shaping moral judgments that deflect responsibility for correcting system flaws onto individuals.

Cognitive Dissonance

Cognitive dissonance is the mental discomfort people feel when they hold two or more conflicting beliefs, values, or attitudes, or when their behaviours contradict their beliefs. Individuals who experience cognitive dissonance may attempt to reduce the discomfort by changing beliefs or behaviours, justifying the inconsistency, or simply ignoring the conflict.

The flat-earthers used a compass as they set out to find the edge of the world. The compass operates on Earth's magnetic field, which is fundamentally tied to the planet's spherical shape. Regarding their contradictory choice of expedition aid, they could be fundamentally ignorant of its scientific significance, or, if they were not, they likely chose to ignore the contradiction in response to the dissonant experience.

Cognitive dissonance helps explain leaders' bewildering responses to the AIDS epidemic. Early ecclesiastical silence reflected the difficulty religious leaders faced in reconciling a moral duty of compassion with doctrines that condemned homosexuality.

Dehumanization

Dehumanisation is a cognitive bias in which we cease to recognise others as fully human, diminishing their capacity for thought, feeling, and moral consideration and allowing us to withdraw concern and even justify their mistreatment. The transatlantic slave trade stands as a primary historical example of systematic dehumanisation, where millions of enslaved Africans were treated as chattel (personal property) rather than human beings. European colonisers often portrayed the natives as inferior, savage, or animalistic and justified their civilising mission, which was, by and large, a violent goal of colonial expansion and profiteering. However, dehumanisation is often subtle, such as when we move or look away from a homeless person. Unable to sit with the discomfort of acknowledging them, we tend to look away and, in doing so, negate their existence.

Political and wartime propaganda often exploits the affect heuristic by flooding audiences with emotionally charged imagery. In the Gaza–Israel conflict, both sides circulated horrifying images to humanise their own victims while emotionally priming audiences to view the other side primarily through acts of violence. The tactic is a two-pronged propaganda: selective humanisation to evoke sympathy or outrage, while dehumanising the opposing community by reducing individuals to labels of evil and cruelty.

Dehumanising bias is also codified into social and legal structures, such as the legal strategy known as the 'trans or gay panic' defence. Defendants attribute their violent assaults against transgender or gay victims to an alleged involuntary panic upon discovering the victim's perceived 'true' identity. This strategy reframes the victim as a provocative catalyst for violence rather than as a human being with an inherent right to life and safety. By casting a person's very existence as threatening, the defence reduces the victim to a dangerous 'other' and shifts moral scrutiny away from the perpetrator's actions.

Dehumanising bias also plays out vividly in modern socio-cultural conflicts. One particular instance was the heated discourse surrounding female athletes perceived to have biological advantages. When Italian boxer Angela Carini abandoned her match against Imane Khelif at the 2024 Paris Olympics, her claims of unfairness ignited a firestorm of controversy. Her claims were rapidly amplified by high-profile figures like J.K. Rowling, who publicly questioned Khelif's gender identity despite her verified status as a biological female by the International Olympic Committee. Carini and Rowling's actions carry a distinct dehumanising quality; they reduce the complexity of the athlete's life to a single, contested biological trait. The incident shows how easily and quickly, to protect our own beliefs, we succumb to dehumanising bias, stripping others of dignity.

20
Emotional Biases

While cognitive biases stem from flaws in our reasoning, emotional biases arise from our feelings and instinctive responses. Strong emotions can overwhelm our ability to think clearly; influenced by our fears, prejudices, and moods, we find it harder to think logically. During emotionally intense moments, our decisions will be driven more by instinct than by rationality. The following biases are often thought processes that individuals rely on in emotionally charged situations.

Loss Aversion

Loss aversion is a cognitive bias in which the pain of losing something is felt more intensely than the pleasure of gaining that same amount. This behaviour was first identified in a controlled study on how individuals perceive their losses and gains. It was the core concept in Prospect Theory, developed by psychologists Daniel Kahneman and Amos Tversky. Both coined the expression 'losses loom larger than gains' to describe loss aversion. That expression aptly describes a common feeling we might have when making personal financial decisions. Whether it is panic selling our stocks or hoarding our savings, both reactions are rooted in our risk-averse nature. In financial markets, an investor might refuse to sell a stock that has lost value, hoping it will recover, even though a more rational decision would be to sell and reinvest the proceeds elsewhere. The investor is avoiding the pain of accepting a loss.

Apart from clinging to losing assets for too long, loss aversion is also attributed to our inertia in ending a failed project or in modifying course from a flawed strategic plan. Abandoning a plan requires us to confront loss or admit failure. That emotional state of confronting losses may be more discomforting than continuing a less optimal endeavour.

Loss aversion is common in consumer behaviour. A store's 'limited time offer' or 'while supplies last' promotion plays on our fear of missing out on a deal, which feels like a loss. Loss aversion could be one of the psychological drivers in SPH Media's misreporting of print media. Rather than confronting the 'painful' reality of a dwindling readership in print media, the culpable protagonists stood by their conviction to misreport higher print circulation figures so they could continue to drive revenue through print media advertising.

Framing Effect

The framing effect is a cognitive bias in which our decisions are influenced by how information or facts are presented, or 'framed' for us. Essentially, when identical information is framed positively (as a gain), it can influence people to make a choice that is distinctively different from when the same information is framed negatively (as a loss). For example, patients are more likely to feel less worried when presented with a high survival rate (80 per cent) for a surgery than with a low mortality rate (20 per cent), even if both rates show the same mortality risk.

The framing effect explains how wording and context can easily alter our perception. A message framed positively and with less risk (or greater certainty) may prompt individuals to adopt a risk-averse stance. In contrast, a negatively framed message may prompt them to adopt a risk-seeking stance. In a study by Kahneman and Tversky, participants were asked to choose between two programs to mitigate a disease expected to kill 600 people. The first two programs were described in positive frames:

- Program A, in which 200 people will be saved.
- Program B, in which the probability of saving people is one-third.

Between program A and B, most people chose the risk-averse option (Program A) because of the certainty of saving 200 lives.

Subsequently, two programs were described in negative frames:

- Program C, in which 400 people will die.
- Program D, in which there is a one-third probability that nobody will die, and a two-thirds probability that they will survive.

Under this framing, most people chose the riskier (or more probable) option because they preferred avoiding the certainty of losing 400 lives.

Advertisers and politicians frequently use the framing effect to sway opinions without changing the facts. Food manufacturers are more likely to use expressions such as 'fat-free' and 'X% fat-free' on their front-of-package labels than a claim like 'low-fat'. A political campaign might focus on 'protecting our jobs' (a positive, lower-risk framing) rather than 'preventing job losses' (a negative, higher-risk frame), even if both phrases address the same issue. The framing effect is also widely used to construct narratives between nations in conflict. The public opinion of the Israel-Gaza war has shifted since the news media began framing the conflict in a different light: from the horrors of terrorism to humanitarian violations, allegedly committed by the Israel Defense Forces.

Affect Heuristic

The affect heuristic is a mental shortcut where our immediate emotional reactions ('affect') guide our decisions and judgments. We commonly describe that decision process or rationale as a 'gutfeel'. Naturally, if we have a positive feeling toward an object, person, or situation, we tend to see only the benefits and downplay the risks. For example, if a company supports a charitable cause we are passionate about, we tend to view its products more favourably. We may even overlook or dismiss any allegations of poor labour practices in that company. Our positive emotional reactions to the company's charity contributions cloud our judgment of its alleged unethical labour practices. In fact, companies often use this cognitive bias to create an emotional 'feel-good' illusion by supporting trending social causes. Sometimes companies leverage consumers' heuristic bias to deflect attention from their ethical problems.

The affect heuristic influences our preference to buy from a brand we feel good about, even if a competitor offers an objectively better product. Thus, food manufacturers often leverage the affect heuristic by using labels that evoke positive feelings about health or ethical practices. Brand names like 'Innocent' and label claims such as 'all natural' are designed to influence our perceptions, sometimes even diverting our attention from the less healthy ingredients in the products. The success of leveraging the affect heuristic effect is evident on supermarket shelves, where processed products with deceptively positive claims often crowd out more nutritious options.

The affect heuristic effect also influences our judgment in negative contexts: our negative feelings steer our focus toward potential dangers, problems, or drawbacks, downplaying any positive aspects. Opposition to school-based LGBTQ+ inclusion policies illustrates the affect heuristic in a negative emotional context. These initiatives were panned as 'indoctrination'. By exaggerating perceived dangers and obscuring well-documented benefits to student well-being, critics trigger fear and moral anxiety among parents. The negative claims gain credibility through emotional resonance.

Negativity Bias

The negativity bias, or negativity effect, is our tendency to place greater weight on negative experiences, thoughts, and information than on positive ones. Bad events and news are more memorable and influential than good ones. This bias can make us overestimate risks, dwell on past mistakes, and be overly cautious. A single critical review, for example, can often have a greater impact on our decision to buy a product than a dozen positive reviews. In relationships, one hurtful comment can overshadow countless acts of kindness. This bias also explains why fearmongering is an effective tactic in politics and the media; stories about crime, disasters, and scandals capture our attention more readily than reports of positive progress. Our minds are instinctively drawn to threats, even when they are statistically improbable.

In the essay on the Paris Olympics, conservative and far-right politicians denounced the opening performance, which involved transgender people, citing its visual resemblance to the Last Supper and its blasphemous intent. They criticised the performance as a desecration of family and religious values; involving transgender performers in the act was, according to them, a deliberate provocation. In their view, the performance was a radical gesture bent on inciting the erosion of social norms. Framing the event as blasphemous could be a cynical tactic to rouse negative reactions to LGBTQ+ activism, associating their drive for diversity and inclusion with socially dysfunctional and disruptive behaviour.

Empathy Gap

The empathy gap is the tendency to underestimate the influence of emotions, both our own and others', on decision-making. We struggle to predict how we'll feel in the future or how someone else's emotional state will affect their choices. For instance, a person might decide to go to a networking event after work, only to find they are too unmotivated when the time comes. We also underestimate how our emotions can lead us to make rash decisions; in a moment of anger, we might send an email we later regret, believing we were in control when we were not. This bias makes it difficult for calm observers to understand decisions made under emotional distress.

During the onset of the COVID-19 pandemic, before any robust work-from-home systems were in place, employees were still required to report to the office. The situation highlighted a profound disconnect, due to an empathy gap, between leadership's focus on business continuity and employees' immediate physical, emotional, and safety concerns amid reports of escalating deaths due to the virus.

The application of the Radiant City vision to France's banlieues also reflects an empathy gap in urban planning. The model prioritised efficiency, order, and functionality, while failing to account for the emotional toll of financial insecurity. Low-income residents often experience chronic stress, insecurity, and a need for dignity. But the initial social housing in France was conceived without regard to residents' need for a sense of belonging, social connection, and economic agency. The result: sterile, disorienting spaces that intensified the very stresses those developments were meant to alleviate.

21
The Seven Mindshifts

From the preceding chapters, we have discovered that cognitive shortcuts are automatic mental processes that enable us to interpret information using past experiences and social cues. Under normal circumstances, these shortcuts allow us to make decisions efficiently. However, their utility falters when we encounter more complex issues, often causing us to deviate from rational thought. When this happens, our perspective becomes tethered to a biased framework that may occasionally result in costly or illogical judgments.

There is no such thing as a 'view from nowhere'. Every piece of information passes through several filters; a 100 per cent bias-free perception is elusive. In fact, attempting to eliminate bias is a quixotic and self-aggrandising pursuit; more often, it only traps us deeper in flawed thinking, reinforced by a sense of self-perceived virtue. Therefore, when we believe we have achieved total objectivity, we are dangerously enlarging our imperception, making ourselves more susceptible to the very prejudices we claim to have eliminated. Nonetheless, improving our metacognition—actively monitoring, regulating, and reflecting on our own thinking processes—can enhance our awareness of biases and help us better manage them.

Enhancing metacognition is an effective approach to mitigating cognitive biases. By practising 'thinking about thinking', we hone the ability to monitor and regulate our thought patterns, thereby enabling us to pause and evaluate information with greater objectivity. The preceding essays in this book serve as a vital catalyst for introspection; they offer a lens for self-inquiry, allowing us to examine cognitive pitfalls so that we may better recognise them in our own thinking. While there is no perfect exit from our labyrinth of biases, fostering this awareness ensures we do not become trapped in a cognitive cul-de-sac of our own making.

Beyond understanding our biases, we must discipline ourselves to adopt habits and mindshifts to minimise their influence on our thinking. In this section, we explore seven active self-checks and philosophical stances to help us refine our reasoning and understand the underlying logics that guide our thinking.

22

A Creature of Context

Cogito ergo sum: 'I think, therefore I am', is René Descartes' renowned quote that established a foundation for modern philosophy, whereby the act of thinking is the single, indubitable proof of our existence. Descartes reasoned that consciousness is the foundation of our existence; even if an external force were to deceive him about the reality of the physical world, the very act of being deceived or doubting was proof of his own existence. Centuries later, artist Barbara Kruger offered a sardonic update to the quote: 'I shop, therefore I am'. The artist rewrote the quote to critique external constructions, specifically how identity is increasingly shaped and affirmed by social signals such as consumption, status, and possessions, rather than by inner reflection.

Both statements shed light on our identity: René Descartes's grounding of existence in thinking, and Barbara Kruger's grounding of existence in material consumption. In different ways, they speak to how identity is understood. Descartes arrived at the *Cogito* by systematically doubting everything he believed until he reached something that could not be questioned: the very act of doubting confirmed that a thinking mind had to exist. While the content of his thoughts could be questioned, the capacity to think, reason, and reflect could not be denied. Extending Descartes' philosophy of doubt, it is worth reflecting on how our thinking is shaped, directed, and framed. Kruger's statement turns the awareness of our existence outward. Rather than beginning with reflection or doubt, she points to a world in which identity is increasingly affirmed through external acts of consumption. Taken together, we can infer that our identity is neither purely internal nor entirely self-constructed; it takes shape between our thinking and the world that surrounds it.

The idea that identity is not fixed but shaped by experience and environment—that we are creatures of context—is well supported by developmental psychology. We learn how to think long before we learn what to think. The early years of life are a period of intense and rapid immersion in contextual learning. Because infants lack the cognitive frameworks and motor control to engage independently with their environment, their learning is necessarily dynamic and reciprocal. From birth, they process information through their five senses, developing cognition not through solitary thinking, but through constant social interaction and the cues they pick up from others.

The psychologist Lev Vygotsky described this as the 'zone of proximal development', where knowledge is not acquired through independent discovery but through social transmission. We become who we are through the mental scaffolding provided by others. Our understanding of right and wrong, of fairness, of affection, even our sensory responses, is inseparable from the environment we are raised in. This idea of contextuality explains why our behaviours are never absolute but conditioned by social and cultural influences. Our reasoning, logic, and even moral judgments are not 'pure' deductions; they are filtered through specific cultural narratives, educational systems, and accumulated experiences. It is through these filters that our initial biases are rooted, quietly hardening into instincts we eventually mistake for facts.

An everyday example of how context shapes us can be found in the way households pass down traditions, particularly through culinary dishes. What one household considers 'authentic' in a dish passed down from a grandparent or elder is highly subjective. For the same dish, recipes from different households often vary widely, ranging from preparation methods and ingredients to unconventional twists. This is because many of these recipes rely on subjective memory; knowledge of how to prepare traditional dishes is often passed down orally or through firsthand experience. Therefore, there are always endless, subtle variations of 'traditional' dishes worldwide, such as Peranakan laksa, Italian bolognese, and tamales. While every household claims to have the authentic recipe, lining up recipes for the same dish would likely reveal distinct methods and ingredient lists. In other words, an authentic recipe is but a contextualised view of truth; each household's method is accepted as authentic, often with little supporting documentation.

Barbara Kruger is among the many creatives in the art world who have extensively explored the social construction of identity. Fashion designers also often express this theme through their collections. Miuccia Prada, along with her collaborators, notably infuses her collections with deliberate design juxtapositions to convey the social construction of gender roles from a woman's standpoint. For instance, Prada's 2023 Spring/Summer collection, titled 'Touch of Crude', featured paper-based dresses torn against the body and refined fabrics with intentional rifts, creases, and untidily stitched hems. Such deliberate imperfections reflect Prada's 'ugly chic' aesthetic and suggest that the notion of 'looking neat' is, at best, a social construct—an ideal imposed on women by society. By purposely incorporating imperfection on a beautiful, high-fashion silhouette, Prada forces both the wearer and the observer to question the social codes of femininity and appropriateness. Prada's approach, ironically, uses the very act of consumption to remind us of the external construction of self, echoing Kruger's critique.

All the above illustrations point to an insight: the self does not develop in isolation but is continuously shaped by the contexts in which it learns, consumes, and belongs. For the same reason, our biases are not the result of deliberate, wilful choices, but often stem from deep-seated societal narratives that unconsciously influence our perspectives and beliefs. When we mistake our subjective view of the world for objective reality, ignoring the filters of our upbringing and environment, we let personal heuristics become universal truths.

By acknowledging and accepting that we are fundamentally shaped and scaffolded by the specific narratives we've been exposed to, we are assuming a crucial mental posture to resist naïve realism and bias. Becoming a creature of context is achieved through intellectual humility, which begins with recognising that our beliefs are limited and no better or truer than those we are unfamiliar with; they are simply perceptions moulded by our surroundings and proximities. When we adopt this mindset, we begin the vital process of examining how our unconscious biases influence our perception and thinking.

23
A Disciple of Experience

We often hear or read about Leonardo da Vinci referred to as the quintessential 'Renaissance Man', a term used to describe someone knowledgeable and talented across many fields, someone who embodies the ideal of intellectual well-roundedness and versatility. To truly understand Leonardo's brilliance, one needs only to browse a handful of pages from his Codex Atlanticus, a 12-volume bound set of drawings and writings housed at the Biblioteca Ambrosiana in Milan. This compilation of more than 1,000 pages spans Leonardo's career from 1478 to 1519. The sheer breadth of his interests and observations, evident even in the few selected pages on display in the gallery, is astonishing: Leonardo recorded everything from engineering sketches and architectural plans to philosophical musings, botanical studies, and even fables. In this single compilation of notes, one may find his designs for canals to improve Milan's transport system, conceptual studies of flying machines, and even a prototype weaving spindle. Besides Codex Atlanticus, Leonardo compiled other scientific manuscripts: the Codex Leicester, his study and observations on the movement of water, its properties, and how it shapes the Earth; and Codex Foster 1 (conserved at the Victoria and Albert Museum). Both are compilations of Leonardo's earliest notebooks, written in his famous mirror writing, on subjects ranging from hydraulic engineering to a treatise on measuring solids. All of his writing reveals a person with wide-ranging inquiry and insatiable curiosity, in a single, remarkably short human lifetime.

Beyond showcasing his work, the extensive volume of his codices reveals fascinating insights into his brilliance: his approach to learning was marked by relentless intellectual curiosity, observation, and experimentation—the very foundation of modern scientific thinking. Unlike many of his contemporaries, Leonardo was not formally educated in the Latin schools of Renaissance Italy. Apart from his basic commercial education from an abacus school, where he learned to keep accounts, he had no classical training. He acknowledged and embraced his lack of formal education with both irony and pride, often signing himself as a 'disciple of experience'—*Leonardo da Vinci, disscepolo della sperientia*—as an affirmation of his self-taught origins and his staunch belief in empirical observation over abstract theory.

Walter Isaacson, renowned for his books on blue-sky thinkers like Albert Einstein, Benjamin Franklin, and Steve Jobs, cited a revelatory passage from one of Leonardo's notebooks in his 2017 biography of Leonardo da Vinci. The written paragraph was a scathing critique of those who dismissed him for being 'unlettered': 'I am fully aware that my not being a man of letters may cause certain presumptuous people to think that they may with reason blame me, alleging that I am a man without learning. Foolish folk! They strut about puffed up and pompous, decked out and adorned not with their own labours, but by those of others. They will say that because I have no book learning, I cannot properly express what I desire to describe, but they do not know that my subjects require experience rather than the words of others.' That quote stands as a testament to his pride in the belief that knowledge may also be gained through direct experience.

Leonardo's passionate, somewhat rebellious retort to those who dismissed him for lacking classical academic training divulged his conviction that learning is best achieved through direct experience and observation. It was a learning process that was deemed unorthodox by the academic norms of his time. A friar's account of his impression of Leonardo, while serving as an intermediary between him and Isabelle d'Este, illustrates how Leonardo's unorthodox approach was often misunderstood. Isabella d'Este commissioned Leonardo to paint her portrait and was frustrated by Leonardo's slow progress; she had repeatedly requested her portrait for about 25 years. According to the friar, Leonardo's lifestyle was 'irregular and uncertain', and he couldn't pin him down. But it was exactly this 'irregular work process' that enabled Leonardo to record thoughts and ideas at random. Some of his ideas were even fantastical at that time, such as the plan to protect Venice with a team of underwater divers wearing breathing apparatus, several centuries before scuba gear came along. Yet beneath this seemingly distracted character was a penetrating thinker who upheld a disciplined and steadfast approach to learning. It was an approach that was structured around several distinctive principles centred on becoming a 'disciple of experience'.

Empirical Learning

As meticulously documented throughout his notebooks and codices, Leonardo's approach to knowledge was profoundly empirical. He believed that direct observation was the most reliable way to acquire knowledge and understand how things truly work. Leonardo's preference for the empirical is also evident in his consistent choice to return to Milan, a city celebrated for its engineers and scientists, rather than the more artistically and classically focused environments of Florence or Rome. His lack of formal academic training might have allowed him to chart an untrodden path of learning grounded in a hands-on, observational approach.

Hands-on experimentation

When Leonardo wanted to understand muscle tension for painting, he dissected corpses. During that experiment, he dissected the body of a 100-year-old man and provided the first description of arteriosclerosis resulting from ageing. Because Leonardo often tested his ideas, he was able to expand and deepen his knowledge of both art and science.

Direct Observation of Nature

Leonardo considered nature his ultimate source of knowledge. Rather than relying solely on books, he viewed the continual discovery of nature as a true path to acquiring and updating knowledge. He vouched for direct observation as a reliable means of contesting and validating facts. His philosophy of observing nature was evident in his wide-ranging studies, from the movements of birds to the curves of the human spine. His approach was prescient, foreshadowing our modern scientific research methods. Leonardo's approach, while lacking a formal methodology, resembled field observation, in which one gathers firsthand accounts of behaviours, interactions, or phenomena for academic research. Just like Leonardo, modern-day field researchers capture unfiltered, in-the-moment details to gather contextual data and probe for insights that might be missed. Embracing this principle means paying attention to ordinary experiences, local conditions, and voices closest to the issue we are investigating. To ensure our actions echo Leonardo's, we have to undertake observing nature.

Profound curiosity

The Codex Atlanticus, Leonardo's largest collection of sketches, diagrams, and handwritten notes, showcases a wide array of subjects including engineering, anatomy, botany, mathematics, astronomy, architecture, and art. This extensive compilation exemplifies his relentless intellectual pursuit, driven by an insatiable curiosity, one that blurs the lines between fields others might consider unrelated.

Interdisciplinary mindset

As observed in his dissections of human bodies to realistically portray muscle tension in paintings, Leonardo saw no division between art and science. He held a mindset that melded his deep curiosity about the natural world with his scientific approach to observation. That interdisciplinary mindset allowed him to paint or record remarkably lifelike, detailed depictions of landscapes, plants, and people. His ability to translate complex optical science into the language of art perfectly illustrates his interdisciplinary capacity. Through the study of optics, he established three core principles: perspective and realism in painting; aerial perspective, which accounts for the blurring of distant objects; and chiaroscuro, the use of light and shadow to create volume. Leonardo's refusal to compartmentalise ideas enabled his pioneering and groundbreaking discoveries.

A collaborative mindset

Despite his earlier scathing remarks about those who dismissed him for lacking a classical education, Leonardo was not a lone genius. His preference for the engineering-focused environment of Milan over the artistically dominated Florence was not without reason. In Milan, he formed a collaborative, professional relationship with the renowned architect Donato Bramante. Both were known to consult and exchange ideas on major court projects. Their working relationship was cordial and marked by a mutual respect for each other's expertise. Leonardo's willingness to learn from and work with individuals outside his primary artistic discipline, such as engineers, artisans, and even military strategists, was a hallmark of his interdisciplinary and collaborative mindset. He understood that true innovation came from the convergence of diverse knowledge and skills.

Walter Isaacson suggests that Leonardo's birth out of wedlock may have worked to his intellectual advantage. Being illegitimate meant he was barred from formal education. Fortunately, Leonardo's lack of formal education spurred his curiosity to roam freely and cross boundaries. As a painter, he used painting as a lens to understand optical theory; as a sculptor, he applied the concepts of form, material, and structure to engineer moving bridges; and as a self-learner, he used his observations to reimagine and hypothesise new ideas and theories.

There is much to emulate in Leonardo's model of learning as we seek to guard against bias. We fall into bias when we think in silos and refuse to question old rules. We eagerly and unknowingly trade the truth for a simple story that explains away a complex problem. By contrast, Leonardo's approach, an interdisciplinary, experimental, and humility-driven quest for knowledge, is the kind of broad-minded inquiry we need to counteract flawed perceptions and systematic errors arising from our cognitive shortcuts.

But no one is truly free from bias, not even great thinkers and geniuses. One of Leonardo's quotes revealed that he, like all mortals, was not an exception: 'The man who has intercourse aggressively and uneasily will produce children who are irritable and untrustworthy,' he wrote, 'but if the intercourse is done with great love and desire on both sides, the child will be of great intellect, witty, lively, and lovable.' A likely motivation for that baseless statement could be his own illegitimacy, or a desire to glorify what his less-than-respected origins. That statement, incongruent with his usual scientific insights, is a reminder that biased views can lurk even in the most self-aware minds. Nonetheless, Leonardo's life achievements show that we can overcome our biases through a disciplined life of expansive learning and intellectual engagement with others. Fostering curiosity, fearlessness in experimentation, and intellectual humility are some mindshift strategies we can adopt to guard against our own biased perceptions.

24

A Collective Defender

We have established that our identity is not fixed but ever-changing, shaped by our personal experiences, thoughts, feelings, and social environment. During our formative years, culture and environment strongly influence the development of our identity, beliefs, perceptions, and thus cognitive shortcuts. Our perceptive lens is therefore inherently biased. Acknowledging that we are creatures of context is a key step toward cultivating an awareness of our internal heuristics. We also discovered that Leonardo's method of learning, which is rooted in experience, observation, and cross-disciplinary curiosity, was an antidote to the authority-driven thinking prevalent in the 15th century. Besides his disciplined approach to learning, he was also a thinker who actively enjoyed and thrived on collaboration. Thinking more clearly requires acknowledging that we are already biased, and, more importantly, a willingness to collaborate with others. The idea that collaboration reduces bias may seem counterintuitive: layering our thinking, already laden with biases, with the perspectives of others who are equally shaped by their own internal heuristics may appear to entangle us in a knotty web of flawed reasoning. Yet meaningful engagement does something subtle: when we deliberate across differences, we are made aware of the limits of our own assumptions. What we perceive as objective truth, even if coherent, may reveal itself as a partial view. Appreciating that tension teaches us that our beliefs and views are not universal truths.

While participating in a group dialogue across differing perspectives can help temper individual bias, we must remain vigilant that it does not drift into conformity and groupthink. Groupthink is one of the most pervasive biases in decision-making, especially within cohesive teams or close-knit communities. Our need for a sense of belonging and our fears of being excluded can conspire to silence our differing views or non-conventional ideas. Nonetheless, I still believe that collaboration, especially with the intention of deliberating across differences, can broaden our thinking, provided it is grounded in openness and a shared commitment to counter biases.

In my first book on cultural leadership, *Staying H.I.R.E.d: The Cultural Kingmaker's Guide to Building Work Oases,* I shared how any individual can proactively foster a collaborative culture by adopting a belief system grounded in four key traits: Humility, Interconnectedness, Resilience, and Empathy. I named my belief system H.I.R.E. My idea of installing a belief system to facilitate a collaborative culture originated in 2015 when my company, 72 Smalldive, embarked on an ambitious expansion into Singapore's retail space.

At that time, the retail sector was facing intense competition from the burgeoning online shopping market, necessitating a transformation in how my physical stores operated. To meet the evolving demands of customers and stay competitive, we faced the significant challenge of hiring and developing a team of retail sales assistants who could think and operate as if they 'owned' the business. This meant finding staff capable of taking ownership to navigate the complexities of evolving retail expectations with confidence and adaptability. We believed that only such employees could help the company stay ahead in the competitive retail market. Despite our efforts to train our employees and provide competitive remuneration and perks, we failed to convey the enthusiasm and inspiration needed to ignite the desired entrepreneurial transformation. My employees continued to resist change at work, preferring to take orders rather than to take the lead. I realised then that no training program, however rigorous, could cultivate ownership if people did not feel genuinely invested in the outcome. And that reckoning prompted me to reassess our approach to training, which necessitated a transformation of my company's organisational culture. That was how a modus operandi and work ethos grounded in the H.I.R.E. belief system was established.

The H.I.R.E. belief system I introduced to my employees was built upon various concepts in organisational strategy. The primary mechanism for achieving a culture of ownership was anchored in the concept of effective followership, coined by Robert Kelly. According to Kelly, a company's success isn't dependent only on leadership and rigorous training; it also depends on team members who take initiative, welcome challenges, and believe their contributions matter. Such team members are what he would call effective followers. On reflection, effective followership is indeed a trait most entrepreneurs possess: a relentless drive to learn, adapt, and evolve amid the dynamic evolution of the businesses they create and lead. Building a team that is capable of taking ownership would require me to foster effective followership within the team; I therefore embarked on a new approach to training, one that I drew inspiration from William Wordsworth's depiction of Lord Nelson in Character of the Happy Warrior and a UC Berkeley Sutardja Centre study on entrepreneurial resilience. That was how a training program centred around the H.I.R.E. belief framework was created.

H.I.R.E. was not introduced as a buzzwordy motivational slogan. It was embedded into my company's structure and daily rhythms. We began by intentionally cultivating psychological safety, creating a modus operandi where questioning assumptions and admitting uncertainty were not penalised but expected. Incentives were redesigned to reward collective wins alongside individual performance, reinforcing the idea that the weakest link in a team was not a liability to distance oneself from, but the most important link to everyone's performance. As a result, stronger performers invested time in coaching those who struggled. At the same time, I shifted from compliance-based training to coaching employees in solution-oriented thinking. They were encouraged to propose remedies before escalating problems, and over time, they began volunteering their ideas and solutions. Through deliberate reflection, adaptability exercises, and explicit norms that protect respectful dissent, humility, resilience, and empathy, these values moved from ethos to actual work behaviours. As these habits took hold, ownership increased, reflected in an 11% rise in sales and a 30% decline in staff turnover. In addition, there was a visible shift in greater initiative and engagement among the employees.

Now, how does the H.I.R.E. belief system effectively curb bias? By embodying these four traits, we foster a psychologically safe environment in which collaboration becomes the default. In a culture anchored by H.I.R.E., flawed ideas or ways of thinking are more likely to surface and be discussed. Humility emboldens us to admit when we are wrong, while an awareness of interconnectedness tempers the 'us vs them' tribalism that so often traps us in our own flawed thinking loop. Resilience increases our tolerance for the discomfort of being challenged, reducing the impulse to rush toward defensive conclusions. And empathy encourages us to listen for understanding. Rather than allowing biases to fester in silence, this framework creates a group dynamic in which individuals feel comfortable questioning assumptions and proposing alternatives without fear of retribution. While no single tool can offer a perfect exit from our cognitive labyrinth of biases, a belief system like H.I.R.E. can serve as a practical, pragmatic organisational framework that helps us anchor on a more expansive view through deliberate collaboration.

25
A Dot Connector

Our immediate association with the phrase 'connecting the dots' is likely the iconic quote from Steve Jobs, delivered in his 2005 Stanford Commencement Address. It is often understood as a disciplined form of introspection. His message, which went viral and inspired many, was a philosophical call to have faith that, if we live with integrity, the threads of our lives will eventually be woven into a meaningful tapestry regardless of the paths we take. For years, I also relied on this concept to guide mentees and coaching clients, encouraging them to reflect on their true and higher purposes as they pursued their goals, thereby bolstering their resilience to overcome the inevitable obstacles they may face. But my version of connecting the dots in this essay does not regard Steve Jobs' philosophy.

Here, I use 'connecting the dots' to refer to a disciplined approach in recognising and questioning the information and patterns that influence our thinking and views. By that, I mean adopting a questioning process in which we deliberately consider diverse perspectives. Ultimately, it is a metacognitive skill that counters bias, resists tunnel vision, and cultivates nuance. To put it simply, my idea of 'connecting the dots' is this: an active discipline of drawing connections between fields of knowledge or seemingly unrelated data points to synthesise new insights. Rather than following a single line of logic, we can step back to see a broader, non-obvious pattern across different domains. The true skill lies in consistently seeking a wider perspective on a derived insight or belief, even when that perspective seems counterintuitive or comes from an entirely different area. The incredible story of how cancer research impacted the AIDS epidemic is a powerful testament to this proactive form of connecting the dots.

A viral cause of cancer was first proposed in 1911 by biologist Peyton Rous. However, during that time, the wider scientific community was sceptical, and Rous's research was largely ignored for nearly 50 years. Although interest in his findings was reignited in the 1960s, a decade-long federal program to identify cancer-causing viruses in humans was terminated in 1980, based on the medical consensus that viruses were not a significant cause of human cancers. But as the AIDS epidemic began, marked by a rising tide of a rare cancer known as Kaposi sarcoma, a handful of researchers re-pursued their research on viral causes of cancer.

One of them was Dr Robert Gallo, who had spent years researching cancer-causing viruses in humans. Gallo's perseverance, amid scepticism from the scientific community, eventually led him to discover HTLV-I. This virus causes a rare form of human lymphoma. His persistence and commitment also led him to prove a retroviral cause for AIDS, which eventually paved the way for the identification of the human immunodeficiency virus (HIV). It was a major milestone as the discovery enabled the development of the first blood test for the virus during the ravaging epidemic. It also laid the groundwork for all subsequent HIV/AIDS therapies. That foundation for Gallo's identification of HIV was actually laid in his cancer research; by joining the information and observations between his research and the symptoms of AIDS patients, Gallo not only proved that viruses could cause cancer but also identified the virus responsible for the AIDS epidemic. Gallo's work on the existence of human retroviruses and their role in disease also laid the conceptual groundwork for an entirely new field: cancer immunotherapy, where a patient's own immune system is leveraged to fight tumours.

Some individuals, like Dr Gallo, appear naturally gifted at connecting the dots; they possess a natural ability to draw relationships between disparate pieces of information in deriving insight. However, the habit of 'connecting the dots' can be cultivated. We can improve our 'dots-connecting' skills by actively strengthening our critical thinking and creative problem-solving. Consider the well-known Five Whys problem-solving technique. It trains us to look past apparent symptoms to uncover deeper root causes by repeatedly asking why. The Five Whys approach to identifying root causes slows our rush to oversimplify.

In the same vein, frameworks such as the TRIZ method and morphological analysis provide the tangible skills needed to 'connect the dots'. The TRIZ method, for instance, provides a framework for thinking that helps us identify contradictions or opposing realities. Similarly, morphological analysis teaches us to break down a phenomenon into its factors, causes, and effects, helping us see its individual components more clearly and avoid oversimplifying complex situations. The above-mentioned problem-solving techniques are not only for engineers; learning and cultivating them as habits of mind can help us gain a broader, more holistic perspective on problems, trends, or phenomena.

Of course, the mere act of joining dots is not enough; we must also adhere to other cognitive principles to avoid chaining ourselves into an erroneous thinking loop. One way is to embrace diverse thinking styles to avoid oversimplifying. Edward de Bono's thinking hats, for example, provide a framework for a more productive, focused, and mindful process. Additionally, we can lean on an evidence-based approach. In an era of unchecked, unvetted information on social media, viewing each piece of information objectively is paramount. Simply asking 'why' without anchoring in facts risks leading us down a path of flawed thinking loops or, even worse, baseless conspiracy theories. More importantly, we should be mindful that connecting dots is just one of many approaches to understanding a phenomenon or observation. The one and only purpose of joining the dots is to discover and consider other causes, circumstances, or alternative explanations to our observations so that we can avoid oversimplifying them.

A truly effective 'dot-joiner' is curious by nature. Without curiosity, we tend to collect dots only within our familiar realms; when we do so, we reinforce existing beliefs rather than challenge them. A curious mind, however, doesn't just seek confirmation; it digs, wanders, and cross-references, seeing connections above noise. In a world drowning in information yet starved of synthesis, our ability to deliberately connect and integrate ideas determines whether we reinforce bias or challenge it; connecting the dots is an important skill in the modern workplace.

26
A Nuanced Inquirer

The mindshifts explored thus far do not reject cognitive shortcuts; they caution against accepting their outputs without scrutiny. In addition to the four mindshifts, nuanced questioning is another approach to refining how we interpret and explain our encounters and observations. To be a nuanced inquirer, we have to be conscious of pausing when an idea or explanation seems too neat, too agreeable, or too easily attributed to a single cause. Nuanced questioning helps us resist the urge to accept simple explanations for what could be complex events.

Our preference for perfectly framed explanations may partly stem from a cultural shift during the Industrial Revolution, which gradually recalibrated our expectations of quality and error. When I first launched my slow-fashion accessory label, 72 Smalldive, I discovered that many customers, accustomed to machine-made precision but unfamiliar with artisanal goods, perceived even natural variations in handcrafted leather as flaws. It is a reflection of how mass production has normalised uniformity, and we have gradually attuned to seeing variation as a defect rather than an inherent quality. The Arts and Crafts movement, led by figures such as William Morris, emerged in part as a protest against this shift. The Arts and Crafts movement was concerned that the pursuit of industrial precision would erode not only craft traditions but also the appreciation for organic irregularity. It was a prescient concern, given that consumers today regard product consistency and uniformity as fundamental pillars of quality and perfection. This view diminishes the perceived value of handcrafted and artisanal goods.

The Industrial Revolution also reframed how we think about error: any deviation from uniformity is considered undesirable and ought to be eliminated. This stance has seeped into how we evaluate information. From the seamless arcs of streaming platforms to hyper-curated social media feeds, we increasingly equate polish with credibility and fluency with truth. However, fluency is not the same as accuracy. A perfectly structured narrative can still be factually thin or even flawed. Constructing a truthful, verifiable understanding of an observation or phenomenon is iterative and rarely reducible to a neat theory or explanation; discernment requires the mindset of a nuanced inquirer.

Nuanced inquirers are not motivated by a preconceived conclusion or ideology. They adopt a disciplined questioning process that acknowledges the fallibility of perceptions, seeks reliable, valid information, and considers contextual influences— historical, socio-cultural, or situational. Nuanced inquirers respect and expect complexity in their discovery. Their world is not binary: economic hardship is rarely the result of a single bad policy, social unrest doesn't stem from a single source of discontent, and solutions to a public health crisis may be found far beyond the healthcare system. Instead of seeking an absolute verdict of truth, nuanced inquirers explore multidimensional perspectives on a single reality.

We have likely all been taught that considering multiple narratives is an effective way to address bias, and most of us would readily acknowledge that reality is polyvocal. Yet awareness alone does not change our thinking habits. We continue to gravitate toward single, coherent accounts of complex events. Part of this pull lies in the cognitive ease they offer. A tightly constructed explanation reduces ambiguity, accelerates decision-making, and creates the reassuring sense that the situation is understood.

When fragmented information is pieced into a seamless narrative, both speaker and listener experience a subtle psychological reward. The listener gains clarity and direction; the speaker gains authority and coherence. But a narrative that feels complete may still be selectively assembled. Single-voiced explanations are not necessarily false, but they could be partial. As nuanced inquirers, we should not mistake polished partiality for totality. We must resist the seduction of premature coherence and learn to tolerate the unfinished edges of understanding, and to do so, here are the mindsets we must wholeheartedly embrace:

Acknowledge Complexity

Rather than rushing toward a single, silver-bullet explanation, we must recognise that most issues arise from multiple causes and will continue to evolve as conditions change. Acknowledging complexity means accepting the presence of opposing views as a reality, and that multiple factors, solutions, and views can simultaneously shape outcomes in ways that are neither linear nor predictable. To acknowledge complexity is also to tolerate ambiguity and resist premature conclusion. To achieve this mind shift, we need to hold our interpretations lightly and remain open to revising them as new information emerges. In this manner, we foster continuous learning, an appreciation for deepening our understanding, and an intellectual maturity centred on remaining open to the possibility that no ready answer is at hand.

Think Slowly

Always define and interpret any phenomenon, problem, or observation thoroughly and slowly. Deliberate questioning calls for slow thinking. We need to invest time in understanding root causes and exploring how surrounding circumstances, or context, give meaning to the reality before us. Applying the five-whys method can help us slow down our thinking process and devote more time to unearthing diverse views, narratives, and reasons.

Deconstruct and Analyse

While connecting the dots helps us grasp an overall picture, deconstructing and analysing requires us to break that picture into its constituent parts. It asks us to move beyond 'what happened' to examine 'how did this unfold?' and 'why did it occur?' By isolating individual elements, tracing their relationships, and scrutinising our assumptions, we may uncover patterns that are otherwise concealed by a superficial narrative.

Take Leonardo da Vinci's experimental learning, for example: to render a human hand realistically, he dissected the hand, studying the bones, muscles, and tendons beneath the skin. By understanding these underlying mechanisms, he could realistically paint the entire hand. In the same way, complex issues demand structural examination. By analysing the causes, constraints, and contexts, we may move closer to a more grounded and comprehensive understanding.

Seek Diverse Perspectives

No single vantage point captures the full comprehension of a complex issue. Actively engaging with people with different lived experiences, disciplines, or interpretive lenses expands our understanding and exposes knowledge gaps in our reasoning. Seeking diverse perspectives refines judgment. To do so effectively, the environment must be psychologically safe for individuals to speak with candour. Attention must also be given to conducting the dialogue respectfully, with intellectual humility, and in a disciplined manner to prevent conversations from trailing off into murmurs. When thoughtfully pursued, diverse perspectives render greater clarity.

Hypothesise and Iterate

Treat our understanding and views as working hypotheses that are subject to validation. With this subtle shift from 'knowing' to 'exploring', we can keep our inquisitive mind alive and prevent our views and perceptions from hardening into dogmas. Rather than seeking definitive answers, the nuanced inquirer advances through provisional interpretations by examining evidence, adjusting assumptions, and refining conclusions as new information emerges. Once again, iteration requires intellectual humility. Each revision acknowledges that earlier interpretations were partial rather than final. When we willingly revisit and recalibrate our views, we build a resilient cognitive foundation, one that evolves alongside the complexity it seeks to understand.

Systems Thinking: See the Whole, Not Just the Parts

Oversimplification often occurs when we detach an issue from the larger realm in which it operates. While deconstructing helps us examine individual causes, seeing the whole requires understanding how those elements interact, reinforce, or constrain one another. Most social and organisational challenges, such as inequality, climate change, or addiction, arise from interdependent factors in force. The nuanced inquirer resists the temptation to treat a single cause as a self-contained explanation and instead places it within the broader scope. A discipline approach to seeing the whole is systems thinking.

We tend to gravitate toward neatly framed explanations because complexity is cognitively demanding and uncomfortable. Systems thinking is a methodical approach that enables us to study an issue beyond the surface and to root out any underlying causes and contexts. Systems thinking involves four principles:

1. Taking a holistic view rather than stripping events from their context.
2. Examining how causes or factors interact, reinforce, or constrain one another.
3. Observing patterns and trends over time instead of focusing solely on isolated incidents.
4. Investigating the underlying dynamics that give rise to observable outcomes.

With this approach, we will become less reactive to readily available narratives but more attentive to interdependencies at play. It is a methodical approach to enhance our perceptions. Because it is a process that does not guarantee perfect explanations, systems thinking helps foster a mindset of steadiness amid uncertainty. With practice, we can become better at resisting oversimplification and more at ease admitting that we do not yet understand enough.

27
An Equanimous Self-Steward

Our emotions are not enemies of our reasoning. In fact, contemporary research in neuroscience and psychology supports the view that emotions are integral to our reasoning and decision-making. In potentially dangerous situations, our emotions enable us to make quick, instinctive assessments necessary for our survival. However, when emotional intensity overrides reflective thinking, our reasoning narrows. We begin to prioritise certainty over clarity. High-emotion situations increase the risk of misjudgment. Fear, pride, excitement, and anger create an internal clamour that demands attention. In such moments, we reach for simplified explanations to avoid discomfort, often at the expense of rational decision-making.

Intense emotions can momentarily dominate our sense of control. When emotions take over, we fixate on them. In emotionally charged states, we default to cognitive shortcuts, making us more vulnerable to bias. Yet emotions are not the enemy. They help us interpret our environment, connect with others, and make meaningful decisions. Suppressing them is neither realistic nor healthy. The real challenge is remaining emotionally aware without allowing emotion to dominate deliberate thought.

Psychologists and neuroscientists discover a complex interplay between our emotions and cognition, in which high emotional intensity disrupts analytical thinking. This response is rooted in the amygdala, an almond-shaped structure central to emotional processing. The amygdala evaluates sensory information, assigns emotional value, and links emotions to our memories. It helps form and consolidate memories of emotionally arousing experiences, ensuring that important events with survival value are remembered. The amygdala may perceive high-emotion situations as threatening. When that happens, it temporarily overrides or impairs our higher-order brain functions such as planning, decision-making, and analysis. In highly stressful situations, the amygdala may also signal the nervous system to release adrenaline and cortisol, which can cause physical discomfort and impede slow, deliberate thinking. This phenomenon is commonly known as an amygdala hijack. In such states, emotion can eclipse our capacity for deliberate reasoning.

An example of fear overwhelming logic is the enduring anxiety about strangers distributing poisoned Halloween candy. Though sociologist Joel Best found no substantiated cases of children being seriously injured by contaminated candy from a stranger, the urban myth instils a potent fear among parents, so much so that some US communities have banned trick-or-treating. This fear-driven, widespread ban in response to the urban myth illustrates how emotional hijacking can often override rational judgment.

Another illustration of how emotion can distort public discourse emerged in the child sexual abuse cases in northern UK towns such as Rochdale and Rotherham. When the news of the abuses was reported, much of the public's attention was on the institutional failure (police and social services) to protect the victims. However, those abuses swiftly became a narrative for extremists to advance an anti-immigrant message. Because some abusers were of South Asian heritage, right-wing parties and groups usurped the storyline, steering the focus from institutional failure to an anti-immigrant and racist agenda. Extremists tapped into public fear and outrage with an accusatory narrative that alleged South Asians migrants were dangerous perpetrators of child sexual exploitation. Those emotionally evocative propaganda against South Asians created a moral panic. So effective is the moral panic that the allegation continues to surface in political discourse to this day. The UK Home Office concluded in 2020 that group-based child sexual exploitation offenders are most commonly white and cautioned against linking ethnicity to these child sexual abuse crimes. Despite that, as recently as 2023, former UK Tory party member Suella Braverman still claimed that child grooming gangs in the UK were 'almost all British Pakistani'. This is yet another illustration of how emotions make us more susceptible to biases.

Although our emotions narrow the aperture through which we perceive situations, avoiding or suppressing them is unhealthy. But we can turn emotional triggers to our advantage, using them as checks on our thought processes. This is because we are less likely to think logically when we are emotional; an emotionally charged state propels us to accelerate our cognitive responses. Emotions influence our decision-making; we tend to rely on cognitive shortcuts rather than engage in critical thinking. In those moments, we should pause and reflect. When we notice a surge of defensiveness, urgency, indignation, or pride, we are likely entering a cognitive danger zone. Such moments call for deliberate self-inquiry: Is my defensiveness filtering out disconfirming evidence? Is urgency pushing me toward premature action? Is moral certainty narrowing how I interpret facts? Is pride preventing me from revising a failing idea?

The equanimous self-steward must be cautious with both positive and negative emotions. Passion, for example, is a highly lauded emotion at work. Though typically seen as positive, passion can also disguise bias. Sometimes, the deeper we care, the more likely we are to dismiss conflicting evidence, resist opposing views, and defend personal ideals. Any feelings or emotions, whether positive or negative, can potentially distort objectivity.

But how do we prevent our emotions from hijacking our thought processes? Using the process of proofing bread dough as an analogy, the best thing to do when we are feeling emotionally charged in a situation is to take a pause. As bread dough must rest before it rises properly, emotionally charged thoughts also require time for a deliberate response; a pause allows us to hold off for a while before replying to a message, delay a decision overnight, or write down our reasoning before acting.

Becoming an equanimous self-steward requires emotional literacy. To possess emotional literacy, we must monitor our feelings and be watchful of their influence on our views. More importantly, we must be able to regulate them. For example, when we are excited about a plan, it may be helpful to pause before executing it. Use that pause to run due diligence, identify knowledge gaps, and consider any other issues we might have overlooked. When we feel fearful about an uncertain outlook, taking a pause again allows us to craft a deliberate action plan to seek clarity. Ruminating in fear would only sink us into self-defeat. The equanimous self-steward uses emotions as a compass to navigate a calmer, more controlled line of thought. When we acknowledge our emotions rather than suppress them, we gradually gain power over them.

28
A Creative Renegade

Artists and creative people possess a powerful, often overlooked trait: the ability to meet challenges and adapt with resilience. As Olivia Laing's incisive biographical essays in *Funny Weather* reveal, most artworks' true existence lies in the intimacy of the artists' struggle: their confrontation with forces such as loneliness, homophobia, or alcoholism, which shape how they think and perceive the world. An artist's work is often a resilient response to adversity. Creativity is, in fact, cognitive elasticity at work. Completing a creative work also requires discipline in refining the artwork through constant iteration. Through intimate self-exploration and rigorous refinement of their creative process, artists nurture adaptability and agility in response to change. I believe, for this reason, the creative journey bestows on one a spirit that tempers rigidity and reduces attachment to a single outcome.

In my meeting with Singaporean ceramicist Iskandar Jalil at his exhibition, he shared that he often discarded pots he had created. He explained his intention for discarding them was to cultivate an emotional detachment from the finished objects, a practice he believed would motivate him to perfect his creations. His approach, like that of many artists mentioned in Olivia Laing's *Funny Weather*, fosters resilience in sustained creation. Jalil's philosophical practice once again proves that for many artists, the process of creation often matters more than the finished work. Artists' cognitive elasticity in adapting, iterating, and refining closely resembles what psychologists describe as a growth mindset.

Creative people and artists also possess a drive and readiness to challenge conventional constraints. Their ability to defy constraints is illustrated in a TED Talk by design critic Alice Rawsthorn about 'design renegades'. Design renegades are figures who dare to tackle the status quo with bold reinvention. The pirate Blackbeard, for instance, was a skilled showman who used his terrifying appearance by tucking lit fuses into his thick, black beard to create smoke and a frightening spectacle and therefore avoided the need for violence. Blackbeard's theatrics and psychological strategy were a form of design: by stoking fear, he ensured naval ships would quickly surrender, allowing his crew to maximise their spoils with minimal casualties.

In her presentation, Rawsthorn also introduced Florence Nightingale, whose renegade act was bridging two seemingly unrelated domains: nursing and mathematics. Nightingale employed her mathematical and statistical knowledge to advise the British Army and government on medical data collection and management. She was most famous for using data and graphs to examine the causes of higher mortality rates among British soldiers than among ordinary British men. Then there was Buckminster Fuller in the 20th Century, renowned for his geodesic dome, which defied architectural tradition and became an efficient and popular design for everything from housing to large exhibition centres. Crucially, Fuller's dome design formula also included instructions for building an emergency shelter from readily available scraps such as wood, metal, plastic, or old blankets. Fuller's design emphasis on resourcefulness and low-cost materials has inspired companies like Pacific Domes to adopt his concept for providing durable shelters in disaster areas and refugee camps. Rawsthorn identified a unifying trait of 'design renegades': they all dare to defy the limiting conditions of their reality.

Because the creative process demands experimentation, revision, and being comfortable with uncertainty, creatives are less hesitant to question conventions. Through constant revision and experimentation, creatives develop habits of openness and adaptability. These habits weaken any attachment to fixed interpretations and outcomes, making it easier for creatives to pursue the unconventional. Bias, by contrast, thrives when we refuse to question the status quo and resist re-examining the familiar. When we adopt a creative mindset, one marked by openness, reinvention, and non-attachment, the hold of cognitive biases on us becomes tenuous.

Leonardo's proud proclamation as the disciple of experience, and his work processes, which yielded many wide-ranging ideas, already hinted at an ethos founded on continual discovery and learning. When we are open to learning, we are more willing to challenge assumptions and thus more resilient to embrace change. We are also more likely to critically evaluate our thought patterns, thereby becoming more aware of filters that influence our perceptions. Becoming a creative renegade, one that accepts impermanence, tolerates ambiguity, and stays curious, is one of the best defences we have against biases. Cognitively flexible and enthusiastically experimental, creative renegades are at ease with the notion that every idea can be reshaped and that even long-trusted beliefs can be revisited and revalidated.

Creative renegades are also very comfortable with non-answers. It is a mindshift that promises a path to deeper intellectual growth. Yet in academic and corporate environments, the impulse to seek definite solutions and decisive explanations is strong. Openness to multiple interpretations or the possibility that no single answer will suffice can be challenging in settings that prize efficiency and certainty. If you aspire to be a creative renegade in such environments, you will need quiet courage to hold space for ambiguity. Imagine yourself as an arthouse film director who intrigues the audience by resisting tidy resolution, inviting interpretation rather than closure, and remaining attentive to nuances. To foster a creative renegade spirit, we have to cultivate an instinct to question, entertain possibilities, and consider multiple perspectives before settling on any judgment. And with consistent practice, we can weaken rigid thinking.

173

Parting Notes

Many of the examples in this book intersect with contemporary political debates. My purpose is to emphasise how all political ideologies are biased. Wherever power is exercised, left-leaning, centre or right-leaning, democratic or otherwise, political actors all adopt a similar persuasive playbook to tap into our cognitive vulnerabilities. Besides political rhetoric, electoral campaigns and messaging also frequently rely on emotionally resonant, simplified narratives to mobilise our attention and loyalty.

Throughout this book, I have drawn on contentious and emotionally charged issues, including debates over gender identity, the Israel–Gaza conflict, and immigration. These subjects were not chosen to advance a particular stance, nor to suggest that one side holds moral superiority over another. My aim in these examples is not to single out a political camp, but to illustrate how easily our reliance on cognitive shortcuts can be triggered, affecting how we selectively interpret, process, or ignore information to maintain a consistent worldview.

There are many books on cognitive biases and countless approaches to understanding them. This book touches on only a small part of how we might better understand the influence of bias in our daily decisions. I hope it scratches the surface and encourages you to explore further.

Many of the issues I have covered are deliberately presented without tidy conclusions; complex matters rarely yield definite answers. By resisting the urge to settle on a final judgment, we allow ourselves to consider multiple perspectives, expand our understanding, and engage with ambiguity. This is precisely the mindset that can help illuminate how our biases shape our thinking.

René Descartes wrote, 'We do not describe the world we see. We see the world we can describe.' If that is so, then expanding our descriptions expands our sight. The hope of this book is modest but sincere: that when confronted with divisive issues, we might feel less compelled to take sides reflexively and more inclined to investigate them by pausing, inquiring, and broadening our perceptions.

Credit, End Notes, and References

Chapter 1

Seren Morris. 'Flat Earthers Quarantined After Taking Wrong Route Trying to Find End of the World.' *Newsweek*, September 01, 2020. https://www.newsweek.com/flat-earthers-quarantined-wrong-route-trying-find-end-world-1528943

Katy Prickett. John Devine. 'The Fens and the flat Earth conspiracy.' *BBC News*, April 18, 2025. https://www.bbc.com/news/articles/c4g3rl97lqpo

Rob Picheta. 'The flat-Earth conspiracy is spreading around the globe. Does it hide a darker core?' *CNN,* November 18, 2019. https://edition.cnn.com/2019/11/16/us/flat-earth-conference-conspiracy-theories-scli-intl

Chapter 2

Andrew Roth. 'Son of CIA deputy director was killed while fighting for Russia, report says.' *The Guardian*, April 25, 2025. https://www.theguardian.com/us-news/2025/apr/25/michael-alexander-gloss-cia-russia

Chapter 3

Owen Walker. 'Rich and naive': why Singapore is engulfed in a 'scamdemic.' *Financial Times,* May 26, 2026. https://www.ft.com/content/3299cf7e-67bd-4654-8aa9-55fc24a66b63

'Singapore improves in OECD ranking of adult skills, but atrophy in literacy a concern' *Nanyang Technological University*, December 10, 2024. https://www.ntu.edu.sg/nie/news-events/news/detail/singapore-improves-in-oecd-ranking-of-adult-skills--but-atrophy-in-literacy-a-concern

'Share of the labour force in Singapore in 2024, by highest educational attainment.' *Statista*, November 9, 2025. https://www.statista.com/statistics/1155893/singapore-share-of-labor-force-by-educational-attainment

David Sun. 'Scammers, recruiters face up to 24 strokes of cane, mules up to 12 strokes under new Bill.' *The Straits Times*, October 14, 2025. https://www.straitstimes.com/singapore/politics/caning-scammers-up-to-24-strokes-for-syndicate-members-recruiters-maximum-12-strokes-for-mules

Chapter 4

Marianna Giusti. 'Everything I, an Italian, thought I knew about Italian food is wrong.' *Financial Times*, March 22, 2023. https://www.ft.com/content/6ac009d5-dbfd-4a86-839e-28bb44b2b64c

Angela Giuffrida. 'Italian academic cooks up controversy with claim carbonara is a US dish.' *The Guardian*, March 27, 2023. https://www.theguardian.com/world/2023/mar/27/italian-academic-cooks-up-controversy-with-claim-carbonara-is-us-dish

Paul Kirby. 'Italy moves to ban lab-grown meat to protect food heritage.' *BBC*, March 29, 2023. https://www.bbc.com/news/world-europe-65110744

'UNESCO nod for hawker food? Not so fast, Malaysians tell Singapore.' *Channel News Asia,* November 6, 2018.
https://cnalifestyle.channelnewsasia.com/world/unesco-nod-hawker-food-not-so-fast-malaysians-tell-singapore-432331

Chapter 5

Christina Pazzanese. 'A decidedly mixed bag.' *The Harvard Gazette,* February 11, 2014.
https://news.harvard.edu/gazette/story/2014/02/a-decidedly-mixed-bag

Chapter 6

'Chinese Restaurant Syndrome - what is it and is it racist?' *BBC,* January 16, 2020.
https://www.bbc.com/news/world-us-canada-51139005

'The palm oil controversy explained.' *Be The Story.*
https://www.be-the-story.com/en/environment/palm-oil-and-the-controversy-behind-it/

Paul Tullis. 'How the world got hooked on palm oil?' *The Guardian,* February 19, 2019.
https://www.theguardian.com/news/2019/feb/19/palm-oil-ingredient-biscuits-shampoo-environmental

'Replacing Trans Fat' *Palm Oil Alliance.*
https://palmoilalliance.eu/replacing-trans-fat

'"Superfoods", a super-impact on the environment.' *British Ecological Society,* April 29, 2020.
https://www.britishecologicalsociety.org/superfoods-super-impact-on-the-environment/

Ainhoa Magrach, María José Sanz. 'Environmental and social consequences of the increase in the demand for 'superfoods' worldwide.' *British Ecological Society,* April 29, 2020.
https://besjournals.onlinelibrary.wiley.com/doi/full/10.1002/pan3.10085

Bee Wilson. 'Protein mania: the rich world's new diet obsession.' *The Guardian*, January 4, 2019. https://www.theguardian.com/news/2019/jan/04/protein-mania-the-rich-worlds-new-diet-obsession

Chapter 7

Tan Si Hui. 'SPH Media files police report after investigation into inflated circulation numbers finds potential offences.' *Channel News Asia,* June 21, 2023.

Chapter 8

Binyamin Appelbaum. 'Sports Stadiums Are Monuments to the Poverty of Our Ambitions.' *The New York Times*, May 28, 2025. https://www.nytimes.com/2025/05/28/opinion/stadiums-sports-nfl-commanders.html

Thomas Fuller. 'How Does Paris Stay Paris? By Pouring Billions Into Public Housing.' *The New York Times,* March 19, 2024. https://www.nytimes.com/2024/03/17/realestate/paris-france-housing-costs.html

Alain de Botton. *The Architecture of Happiness*. United Kingdom: Penguin, 2006. https://www.alaindebotton.com/architecture/

Growth-Fueled Biases

David Marchese. 'This Pioneering Economist Says Our Obsession With Growth Must End.' *The New York Times*, July 17, 2022. https://www.nytimes.com/interactive/2022/07/18/magazine/herman-daly-interview.html

Chapter 9

Bernardo Mueller, João Gabriel Ayello. 'How the East was Lost: Institutions and Culture in 16th Century Portuguese Empire.' *Dept. of Economics Universidade de Brasilia*, August 19, 2025. January 2020. https://economics.yale.edu/sites/default/files/how_the_east_was_lost_aug_26_2016.pdf

'Spanish-American War' *Britannica*, January 9, 2026.
https://www.britannica.com/event/Spanish-American-War

'Indian Rebellion of 1857' *Britannica*.
https://www.britannica.com/event/Spanish-American-War

Rajib Lochan Sahoo. 'Indian Cotton Mills and The British Economic Policy, 1854-1894.' *Proceedings of the Indian History Congress*. Vol. 76, 2015: 356-367.
https://www.jstor.org/stable/44156602

Chapter 10

Jon Henley. 'It was like us – a chaotic mess: France enjoys Paris Games opening ceremony.' *The Guardian*, July 27 19, 2024.
https://www.theguardian.com/world/article/2024/jul/27/france-verdict-paris-olympic-opening-ceremony

Jon Henley. 'Olympic 'Last Supper' scene was in fact based on painting of Greek gods, say art experts.' *The Guardian*, July 29 19, 2024.
https://www.theguardian.com/sport/article/2024/jul/29/olympic-last-supper-scene-based-painting-greek-gods-art-experts

'Olympic chiefs 'sorry' opening ceremony caused offence.' *BBC*, July 28, 2024. https://www.bbc.com/sport/olympics/articles/cw4yqvegkexo

Steven McIntosh. 'DJ files complaint over opening ceremony abuse.' *BBC*, July 30, 2024.
https://www.bbc.com/news/articles/c0xj358y7n5o

Alexandra Fouché. 'Death threats against Olympics organisers investigated.' *BBC*, August 4, 2024.
https://www.bbc.com/news/articles/c9e997g3xr1o

Ines Eisele. 'Fact check: Do trans women have unfair athletic advantage?' *DW*, March 20, 2025. https://www.dw.com/en/do-trans-women-have-an-unfair-athletic-advantage/a-58583988

Kara Swisher. 'Martina Navratilova on Why She Keeps Talking About Trans Women in Sports?' *New Yorker*, November 30, 2023.
https://nymag.com/intelligencer/2023/11/on-with-kara-swisher-navratilova-on-trans-women-in-sports.html

Chapter 11

Nicholas Kristof. 'How to Think Through the Moral Tangle in Gaza.' *The New York Times,* June 1, 2024.
https://www.nytimes.com/2024/06/01/opinion/israel-gaza-antisemitism.html

Rhea Yasmine. 'Singapore must never allow divisive rhetoric to erode mutual respect and unity: Faishal Ibrahim' *The Straits Times*, May 24, 2025.
https://www.straitstimes.com/singapore/spore-must-never-allow-divisive-rhetoric-to-erode-mutual-respect-and-unity-faishal-ibrahim

'Why is Israel launching a crackdown in the West Bank after the Gaza ceasefire?' *PBS,* January 22, 2025.
https://www.pbs.org/newshour/world/why-is-israel-launching-a-crackdown-in-the-west-bank-after-the-gaza-ceasefire

Emma G. Fitzsimmons, Lauren Hirsch. 'Mamdani Says He Will Discourage the Term Globalise the Intifada.' *The New York Times,* July 15, 2025.
https://www.nytimes.com/2025/07/15/business/mamdani-globalize-intafada-business-leaders.html

James Pamment, Vladimir Sazonov, Francesca Granelli, Sean Aday, Māris Andžāns, Una Bērziņa-Čerenkova, John-Paul Gravelines, Mils Hills, Irene Martinez-Sanchez, Mariita Mattiisen, Holger Molder Yeganeh Morakabati, Aurel Sari, Gregory Simons, Jonathan Terra. 'Hamas' use of human shields in Gaza.' *NATO StratCom COE,* June 6, 2019.
https://stratcomcoe.org/cuploads/pfiles/hamas_human_shields.pdf

Khaled Elgindy, Eyal Lurie-Pardes. 'Human shields or shielding Israel from accountability?' *Middle East Institute*, May 10, 2024.
https://mei.edu/publication/human-shields-or-shielding-israel-accountability/

Deborah Cole. 'German position on Israel-Gaza debate putting artists off film festival.' *The Guardian*, December 16, 2024. https://www.theguardian.com/film/2024/dec/16/berlin-film-festival-berlinale-tricia-tuttle-israel-gaza

'What Does "Globalise the Intifada" Mean and How Can it Lead to Targeting Jews with Violence?' *American Jewish Community*, December 18, 2025. https://www.ajc.org/news/what-does-globalize-the-intifada-mean-and-how-can-it-lead-to-targeting-jews-with-violence

Leila Molana-Allen. 'Palestinian Authority not going to Gaza on an Israeli military tank PM says.' *PBS*, Nov 6, 2023. https://www.pbs.org/newshour/show/palestinian-authority-not-going-to-gaza-on-an-israeli-military-tank-pm-says

Tom McArthur, Jon Donnison.'Israeli settlement plans will 'bury' idea of Palestinian state, minister says.' *BBC*, August 14, 2025. https://www.bbc.com/news/articles/ckgdzxpkdd7o

'Israel approves military takeover of Gaza City.' *BBC Global News Podcast*, August 8, 2025. https://www.bbc.com/audio/play/p0lvxswh

Emir Nader. 'Israeli rights groups accuse Israel of genocide in Gaza.' *BBC*, July 28, 2025. https://www.bbc.com/news/articles/c776xkvz6vno

'Mass Starvation Warnings in Gaza' *BBC*, July 24, 2025. https://www.bbc.com/audio/play/p0ls4b88

'How did Gaza get to the brink of starvation?' *BBC*, July 29, 2025 https://www.bbc.com/news/videos/cjey0v4xjz9o

'In Gaza, mounting evidence of famine and widespread starvation' *UN News*, July 29, 2025. https://news.un.org/en/story/2025/07/1165517

Emma Graham-Harrison. 'The mathematics of starvation: how Israel caused a famine in Gaza.' *The Guardian*, July 31, 2025. https://www.theguardian.com/world/2025/jul/31/the-mathematics-of-starvation-how-israel-caused-a-famine-in-gaza

'Germany suspends arms exports to Israel for use in Gaza.' *DW*, August 8, 2025.
https://www.dw.com/en/germany-suspends-arms-exports-to-israel-for-use-in-gaza/a-73569858

'Woman wearing Palestine Action T-shirt arrested.' *BBC*, August 9, 2025
https://www.bbc.com/news/articles/c5ylp59we55o

Mariam Issimdar. 'Demonstrators arrested at Palestine Action event.' *BBC,* August 16, 2025.
https://www.bbc.com/news/articles/c1dxz9px2v1o

Jennifer McKiernan. 'Some don't know the full nature of Palestine Action, says Cooper.' *BBC*, August 12, 2025.
https://www.bbc.com/news/articles/cj0yyvj7jmmo

Guy Lambert. 'Novelist Sally Rooney says she will support Palestine Action despite ban.' *BBC*, August 17, 2025.
https://www.bbc.com/news/articles/cp94jz0y7ygo

Yvette Cooper. 'Yvette Cooper: Palestine Action is not lawful protest.' *The Observer*, August 17, 2025.
https://observer.co.uk/news/opinion-and-ideas/article/palestine-actions-violent-criminality-is-not-lawful-protest

Chapter 12

Suzanne Goldenberg. 'Exxon knew of climate change in 1981, email says — but it funded deniers for 27 more years.' *The Guardian*, July 8, 2015.
https://www.theguardian.com/environment/2015/jul/08/exxon-climate-change-1981-climate-denier-funding

Oliver Milman. 'Revealed: Exxon made breathtakingly accurate climate predictions in 1970s and 80s.' *The Guardian*, January 17, 2023.
https://www.theguardian.com/business/2023/jan/12/exxon-climate-change-global-warming-research

Suzanne Goldenberg. 'Rockefeller family tried and failed to get ExxonMobil to accept climate change' *The Guardian*, March 27, 2015.
https://www.theguardian.com/environment/2015/mar/27/rockefeller-family-tried-and-failed-exxonmobil-accept-climate-change

Phoebe Keane. 'How the oil industry made us doubt climate change.' *BBC*, September 20, 2020.
https://www.bbc.com/news/stories-53640382

Georgina Rannard. 'ExxonMobil: Oil giant predicted climate change in 1970s – scientists.' *BBC*, January 12, 2023.
https://www.bbc.com/news/science-environment-64241994

'ExxonMobil Abandons Discussions to Develop Expensive Indonesian Gas Field.' *Oil and Gas 360*, July 19, 2017.
https://www.oilandgas360.com/exxonmobil-abandons-discussions-develop-expensive-indonesian-gas-field/

'ExxonMobil's response.' *Business and Human Rights Center*, July 28, 2015.
https://www.business-humanrights.org/en/latest-news/exxonmobils-response

'Union of Concerned Scientists report says fossil fuel industry knowingly worked to deceive public about realities & risks of climate change.' *Business and Human Rights Center*, July 28, 2015.
https://www.business-humanrights.org/en/latest-news/union-of-concerned-scientists-report-says-fossil-fuel-industry-knowingly-worked-to-deceive-public-about-realities-risks-of-climate-change/

'The Climate Deception Dossiers.' *Union of Concerned Scientists*,
July 29, 2015.
https://www.ucs.org/resources/climate-deception-dossiers

'Former Exxon Employee Says Company Considered Climate Risks as Early as 1981.' *Union of Concerned Scientists*, July 8, 2015.
https://www.ucs.org/about/news/exxon-weighed-climate-risks- early-81-companies-misled-public-decades-new-report-finds

Geoffrey Supran, S Rahmstorf, Naomi Oreskes. 'Assessing ExxonMobil's global warming projections.' *Science*, January 13, 2023.
https://www.science.org/doi/10.1126/science.abk0063

Geoffrey Supran, Naomi Oreskes. 'Addendum to 'Assessing ExxonMobil's climate change communications (1977–2014)' *IOP Science*, August 23, 2017.
https://iopscience.iop.org/article/10.1088/1748-9326/aa815f

Chapter 13

Saikou Jammeh. 'Africa Is Big, and It Wants the World's Maps to Show It' *The New York Times*, August 19, 2025.
https://www.nytimes.com/2025/08/19/world/africa/africa-map-mercator.html

'Operation Persil' *Wikipedia*.
https://en.wikipedia.org/wiki/Operation_Persil

Ndongo Samba Sylla , Fanny Pigeaud , Chris Dite. 'Africa: How France Continues to Dominate Its Former Colonies in Africa.' *Committee for the Abolition of Illegitimate Debt*, 26 April 2021.
https://www.cadtm.org/Africa-How-France-Continues-to-Dominate-Its-Former-Colonies-in-Africa

Carl Müller-Crepon. 'Continuity or Change? (In)Direct Rule in British and French Colonial Africa.' *Cambridge University Press*, June 19, 2020.
https://www.cambridge.org/core/journals/international-organization/article/abs/continuity-or-change-indirect-rule-in-british-and-french-colonial-africa

Ali Vitali, Kasie Hunt, and Frank Thorp V. 'Trump referred to Haiti and African nations as 'shithole' countries.' *NBC News*, January 11, 2018.
https://www.nbcnews.com/politics/white-house/trump-referred-haiti-african-countries-shithole-nations-n836946

Zachary B Wolf. 'Americans voted for Trump. Did they vote for this?' *CNN*, January 13, 2025.
https://edition.cnn.com/2025/02/13/politics/americans-support-for-trump-what-matters/index.html

Patricia Cohen. 'How West Africa Can Reap More Profit From the Global Chocolate Market' *The New York Times*. September 28, 2023.
https://www.nytimes.com/2023/09/28/business/economy/ghana-cocoa-fairafric.html

James Crawford-Smith. 'Why Prince William Should Watch Harry's Latest Drama Carefully' *Newsweek*. February 3, 2024.
https://www.newsweek.com/prince-william-watch-prince-harry-latest-drama-carefully-africa-charity-1865925

Lazara Marinkovic. 'Refugees stranded on Serbia-Hungary border amid winter.' *Al Jazeera*, January 13, 2017.
https://www.aljazeera.com/gallery/2017/1/13/refugees-stranded-on-serbia-hungary-border-amid-winter

Chapter 14

Tasleem J Padamsee. 'Fighting an Epidemic in Political Context: Thirty-Five Years of HIV/AIDS Policy Making in the United States.' *Social History of Medicine*, Volume 33, Issue 3, August 2020.
https://academic.oup.com/shm/article/33/3/1001/5265310#221593622

Robert Mills. 'Derek Jarman's Revelation: AIDS, Apocalypse and History.' *Imagining The Apocalypse: Art And The End Times*.
https://courtauld.ac.uk/research/research-resources/publications/courtauld-books-online/apocalypse/derek-jarmans-revelation-aids-apocalypse-and-history/

Justin Parkinson. 'Aids campaign: Thatcher 'fought against risky sex warnings.' *BBC*, February 8, 2021.
https://www.bbc.com/news/uk-politics-55973726

Paul Jerusalem. 'The Forgotten History of the AIDS Epidemic in Singapore.' *Rice Media*, September 15, 2022.
https://www.ricemedia.co/the-forgotten-history-of-the-aids-epidemic-in-singapore/

Rich Barlow. 'How the AIDS Crisis Became a Moral Debate.' *BU Today*, December 3, 2015.
https://www.bu.edu/articles/2015/anthony-petro-after-the-wrath-of-god/

Matthew Tontonoz. 'When AIDS Was a Cancer.' *The Cancer Research Institute Blog*, August 8, 2014.
https://www.cancerresearch.org/blog/when-aids-was-a-cancer

'A Timeline of HIV and AIDS.' *HIV.gov.*
https://www.hiv.gov/hiv-basics/overview/history/hiv-and-aids-timeline

Jacqueline A. Ortiz. 'Silence From the Great Communicator: The Early Years of the AIDS Epidemic Under the Reagan Administration.' *Swarthmore Undergraduate History Journal*, 2023.
https://works.swarthmore.edu/suhj/vol4/iss2/6

Tessa Wong. '377: The British colonial law that left an anti-LGBTQ legacy in Asia.' *BBC*, June 29, 2021.
https://www.bbc.com/news/world-asia-57606847

Chapter 15

Aja Barber. 'The Shein influencer debacle exposed a very ugly truth about fast fashion.' *MSNBC*, Jul. 2, 2023.
https://www.msnbc.com/opinion/msnbc-opinion/shein-instagram-tiktok-influencer-backlash-exposes-fast-fashion-dark-s-rcna92088

Emilio Parodi, Elisa Anzolin, Denis Balibouse, and Mimosa Spencer. 'How migrant workers suffered to craft the 'Made in Italy' luxury label.' *Reuters*, September 18, 2024.
https://www.reuters.com/world/europe/how-migrant-workers-suffered-craft-made-italy-luxury-label-2024-09-18/

Emilio Parodi. 'Classic cashmere purveyor Loro Piana placed under court monitoring over worker abuse.' *Reuters*, July 14, 2025.
https://www.reuters.com/business/retail-consumer/lvmhs-loro-piana-put-under-court-administration-italy-over-labour-exploitation-2025-07-14/

'Inside Italy's designer bag sweatshops | 101 East Documentary.' *Al Jazeera*, 21 November, 2024.
https://www.youtube.com/watch?app=desktop&v=owXegVj1NC4

'Italian fashion house Loro Piana put under court administration.' *Le Monde with AFP*, July 15, 2025.
https://www.lemonde.fr/en/economy/article/2025/07/15/italian-fashion-house-loro-piana-put-under-court-administration_6743394_19.html

Charlotte Edwards. 'Shein suppliers still work 75-hour weeks.' *BBC Business*, May 12, 2024.
https://www.bbc.com/news/articles/cg67w73nxqxo

Florian Blummer. 'Labour dispute at Montblanc: We're not disposable goods.' *Public Eye*, April 8, 2025.
https://www.publiceye.ch/en/topics/fashion/labour-dispute-at-montblanc-were-not-disposable-goods

Chapter 16

Matthew D. Lassiter, Susan Cianci Salvatore. 'Civil Rights in America Racial Discrimination in Housing.' *The National Historic Landmarks Program Cultural Resources National Park Service US Department of the Interior Washington, DC*, March 2021.
https://planning.dc.gov/sites/default/files/dc/sites/op/publication/attachments/Civil_Rights_Housing_NHL_Theme_Study_final.pdf

Matthieu Gimat, Manon Le Bon-Vuylsteke, Bruno Marot, and translated by Oliver Waine. 'Have Low-Income Households Been Failed by the Sale of Social Housing? Three European Experiences Compared.' *Metro Politics,* January 6, 2023.
https://metropolitics.org/Have-Low-Income-Households-Been-Failed-by-the-Sale-of-Social-Housing.html

Philip Oltermann. 'The social housing secret: how Vienna became the world's most livable city.' *The Guardian*, January 10, 2024.
https://www.theguardian.com/lifeandstyle/2024/jan/10/the-social-housing-secret-how-vienna-became-the-worlds-most-livable-city

Francis Newton. 'Brunswick Centre | London.' *The Academy of Urbanism,* March 5, 2018.
https://www.academyofurbanism.org.uk/brunswick-centre-london

Owen Walker. 'Singapore's public housing model meets the limits of its success' *Financial Times*, January 31, 2026.
https://www.ft.com/content/2333c0fc-32df-41d5-9696-ed2d90181c7a?syn-25a6b1a6=1

Chapter 17

'The affair of the diamond necklace, 1784-1785.'
https://en.chateauversailles.fr/discover/history/key-dates/affair-
diamond-necklace-1784-1785

'The necklace that ruined Marie Antoinette? Unboxing the Sutherland
Diamonds.' *Victoria and Albert Museum*, November 11, 2025.
https://www.vam.ac.uk/articles/the-necklace-that-ruined-marie-
antoinette-unboxing-the-sutherland-diamonds

'Affair of the Diamond Necklace.' *Wikipedia*.
https://en.wikipedia.org/wiki/Affair_of_the_Diamond_Necklace

Chapter 23

Walter Isaacson. *Leonardo da Vinci*. United States of America: *Simon &
Schuster*. October 2, 2018
https://www.simonandschuster.com/authors/Walter-Isaacson/697650

Chapter 27

'Rotherham abuse scandal: How we got here' *BBC*, June 22, 2022.
https://www.bbc.com/news/uk-england-south-yorkshire-61868863

Geraldine McKelvie. 'The UK's 15-year scandal no government has
gripped: grooming gangs explained.' *The Guardian*, October 25, 2025.
https://www.theguardian.com/uk-news/2025/oct/25/hugely-wasted-
opportunity-timeline-uk-grooming-gangs-inquiry

Sam Francis, Henry Zeffman. 'Starmer attacks those 'spreading lies' on
grooming gangs.' *BBC*, January 6, 2025.
https://www.bbc.com/news/articles/c75wp53vk1lo

Kenan Malik. 'The right is trying to rewrite history with its toxic rhetoric on
Britain's rape gangs.' *The Guardian*, Jan 12, 2025.
https://www.theguardian.com/commentisfree/2025/jan/12/the-right-is-
trying-to-rewrite-history-with-its-toxic-rhetoric-on-britains-gangs

Jim Waterson. 'Braverman's claim about ethnicity of grooming gangs was false, regulator rules.' *The Guardian*, September 23, 2023.
https://www.theguardian.com/politics/2023/sep/28/braverman-ethnicity-child-grooming-gangs-false-mail-on-sunday

Chapter 28

Alice Rawsthorn. 'Pirates, nurses and other rebel designers.' *TED*, February, 2016.
https://www.ted.com/talks/alice_rawsthorn_pirates_nurses_and_other_rebel_designers

Olivia Laign. *Funny Weather*. United Kingdom: Picador, April 29, 2021.
https://www.olivialaing.com/funny-weather

About The Author

Soh Sze Tiong is a writer, entrepreneur, and organisational thinker whose work examines how human judgment, bias, and culture quietly shape the way we lead and work together. He is the founder of 72 Smalldive, Singapore's pioneer slow-fashion label. He brings over two decades of strategy consulting experience, advising Fortune 500 companies and financial institutions across Europe and Asia, including Sony, GE Medical, Royal Bank of Scotland, and ANZ.

He is the author of *Staying H.I.R.E.d: The Cultural Kingmaker's Guide to Building Work Oasis, in which* he explored ownership, followership, and the conditions needed for healthy organisational cultures. In *Of Flat Earth and Protein Mania, Decoding Our Labyrinth of Biases*, he turns his attention to the invisible architecture of thought—how cognitive shortcuts, emotional reactions, and social narratives can distort perception, complicate leadership, and shape collective outcomes.

Sze Tiong believes that building effective cultures without understanding our inherent biases is a quixotic pursuit; that better leadership begins with metacognition, the ability to examine how we think before deciding how we act. Based between Singapore and Milan, he is a lifelong learner with a deep appreciation for nature, art, and films.

About Two Frappes Books

Two Frappes Books is a publishing project dedicated to providing practical guides and actionable insights for your learning and development journey. Our mission is to offer printed books on useful, actionable content packed with modern cognitive wisdom for working professionals and business owners at a price that won't bat an eyelid—just costing you two Frappuccinos! *Of Flat Earth and Protein Mania* is our second title.

Further Reading by the Author

Staying H.I.R.E.*d*
The Cultural Kingmaker's Guide to Building Work Oasis

In an era of complexity, burnout, and fragmented teams, thriving workplaces are no longer built by hierarchy or control, but by individuals who understand how culture truly forms. *Staying H.I.R.E.d* introduces the idea of the 'cultural kingmaker'—transformative individuals who shape their work environments from the ground up by influencing mindsets, behaviours, and shared values.

Drawing from real-world experience building teams and organisations, the book presents the H.I.R.E. framework—Humility, Interconnectedness, Resilience, and Empathy—as a practical lens for cultivating ownership, effective followership, and collaboration. Rather than prescribing rigid leadership models, it shows how everyday actions and decisions accumulate into cultures that either constrain or enable human potential.

Written for business owners, professionals, and organisational leaders, *Staying H.I.R.E.d* offers a grounded approach to creating work oases— environments where individuals find meaning in their contributions and teams perform with trust, clarity, and purpose.

Continue The Conversation

The author welcomes opportunities to discuss further the ideas explored in these pages, whether through talks, facilitated discussions, or deeper organisational work on leadership, culture, and decision-making.

Readers who wish to continue the inquiry in writing may find related essays on the author's Substack, Yours Slowly Sze (https://szetiong.substack.com), where relevant themes are explored in greater depth in the section EvoluMind.

For speaking engagements, workshops, or direct correspondence, please contact: **twofrappes@72Smalldive.com**